*H. M. Drucker
and
Gordon Brown*

LONGMAN
London and New York

LONGMAN GROUP LIMITED London

Associated companies, branches and representatives throughout the world

Published in the United States of America by Longman Inc., New York

First published 1980

BRITISH LIBRARY CATALOGUING IN PUBLICATION DATA

Drucker, Henry Matthew
  The politics of nationalism and devolution.
  – (Politics today).
  1. Decentralization in government – Great
Britain 2. Scotland – Politics and government
– 20th century 3. Wales – Politics and
government
I. Title II. Brown, Gordon
III. Series
354'.41'082   JN329.D43   79-41025
ISBN 0-582-29520-3

Set in 10/11pt Comp/Set Plantin
Printed in Great Britain by
Richard Clay (The Chaucer Press) Ltd, Bungay, Suffolk

CONTENTS

EDITORS' PREFACE

There is a demand among the general public as well as from students for books that deal with the main issues of modern British politics in such a way that the reader can gain a reliable account of how an issue arose, of its institutional context and then, but only then, to have argument about what should be done.

Behind what have become political issues, there are fundamental problems. Many books identify these problems theoretically, but too often ignore the empirical context, and others are so polemical and doctrinaire, that their conclusions, however just, are distrusted by shrewd readers. We believe in casting out neither facts nor values, but in relating them closely but distinctly. The test of a good book on political issues should be that a reader will feel that he has a full and reliable account of how the issue arose and what institutions and groups affect and are affected by it, irrespective of what the author thinks should be done. But authors cannot just describe, inevitably they prescribe; so let it be done openly and clearly. Politics is too important for neutrality, but therefore demanding of objectivity. So we ask the authors in this series to organise the books into three parts: the recent history of the matter, the institutional setting, and argument about the future.

We believe that relevant books are wanted, neither wholly committed books nor those that pretend to scientific objectivity. This series continues work that we began with Fontana Books, in their 'Political Issues' series, a few titles of which are still to appear. Some similarities will be obvious, particularly in our injunction to authors to write at the highest possible level of intelligence but to eschew all jargon and technicalities. Students of politics should accept, not worry, that they have a public role.

Bernard Crick and *Patrick Seyd*

AUTHORS' PREFACE

Early drafts of this book have been read by Dennis Balsom, Andrew Bolger, Carol Craig, Nancy Drucker, Grant Jordan, Tom Nairn, Jim Naughtie and John Osmond. We are grateful to them for their helpful comments. We want too to thank Bernard Crick and Pat Seyd for standing by us and seeing the book through publication. The text has been typed over and over again by Mona Bennet, Helen Ramm and Jean Tucker, to whose forbearance and care we are much indebted. Nigel Griffiths has helped us check sources. We also wish to thank David Donald, Nigel Griffiths and Stephan Kendrick. Responsibility for the book rests jointly with the authors but readers may wish to know that Part I was originally drafted by Gordon Brown and Parts II and III by Henry Drucker.

We are grateful to the following for permission to reproduce copyright material:
Centre for the Study of Public Policy for a Table from *The United Kingdom as a Multi-National State* by R. Rose; Macmillan, London and Basingstoke for a Table p. 466 from *Political Change in Britain* by D. Butler and D. Stokes.

POLITICS TODAY

General Editors: *Bernard Crick, Patrick Seyd*

POLITICAL ISSUES IN MODERN BRITAIN
Published by Fontana

Part one
THE CONTEXT

Chapter one
THE DISTINCTIVENESS OF SCOTLAND AND WALES

I

Socially, Britain is still a surprisingly homogeneous country. Disparities of economic opportunity and social provision between the regions are of less significance than in many other countries. Britain has neither the concentrations of growth in its metropolitan regions that characterise, say, France, nor the contemporary problems of rural depopulation and decay of, say, Southern Italy. Standards of social welfare are more or less uniform throughout the country and while there are marked differences in regional unemployment rates, these are not as large as in other countries and occupational wage rates are relatively even throughout the land.

Relative social homogeneity has been reinforced by a unitary legislative and administrative system and by a uniformity of political loyalties. It has been commonly argued that industrialisation and the diffusion of its benefits to all areas and groups in the country have minimised the political importance of conflicts between city and country, centre and periphery and official and non-conformist religions. According to the findings of one comparative international study in 1965, Britain had the most class-based political system in Europe, ahead of Sweden, Norway, Denmark, France, Austria and Italy. Britain had no specifically agrarian or rural party such as existed in Switzerland or Finland. It had no party based principally on artisans or the self-employed as in, say, France. It had no political groupings based exclusively on religion as in Switzerland, Belgium, Italy and the Netherlands, and no strong nationalist or secessionist movement flourished in its peripheral areas.

The homogeneity of Britain has, however, always been relative, never absolute. Britain has always been a multi-national state in which national identities have survived. The development of political parties and loyalties around the differing British nationalities has always been possible. Cultural and religious traditions have given Scottish and Welsh life, in particular, a different and distinctive character, and recently it has become clear that there is an economic imbalance between Scotland and Wales and the rest of Britain.

Yet there are divisions too within Scotland and Wales. Scotland can be described as two nations. Its five million people are divided between an over-populated, industrialised central belt – much of whose industry is now decaying – which contains four-fifths of the Scots population, and the rest of the country which, with the exception of Dundee and Aberdeen, is predominantly rural. The industrial areas of Scotland have twice the population density of the UK as a whole, while, by contrast, its rural areas have but one quarter of the UK density. In Wales, which has 2,500,000 people, the difference between the urban industrial mining valleys to the south and the rural farming areas is equally marked. 70 per cent of Welshmen live in only three of the country's eight counties. So great, indeed, are the differences between the industrialised south and the rural north that the national Eisteddfod, the symbol of Welsh nationhood, has to vary its annual meeting place between North and South Wales. Wales is also divided by language with English in the south and Welsh in the north. Whatever its failings, one blessing of the British constitution has been to prevent these social differences within Scotland and Wales from being exacerbated as they might have been if each grouping had had its own political party. Furthermore the social differences between the working and middle classes in both Scotland and Wales are more accentuated than in England.

The strength of Scottish and Welsh identity has, however, rarely been doubted – even if it is exhibited to the outside world most often on the football and rugby fields. The Kilbrandon Commission on the Constitution of 1968–73 accepted Scottish and Welsh nationhood as a fact and their survey of national opinion confirmed that Scots and Welsh people tend to think of themselves as Scottish and Welsh first. The Commissioners concluded:

Our terms of reference refer to the several countries, nations and regions of the United Kingdom and thus appear to accept the claims to separate national identity made on behalf of the Scottish and Welsh peoples. The many discussions we have had with the Scots and the Welsh have given ample evidence of the existence of this sense of nationhood often strongly felt even by those who have no desire to see much change in the existing arrangements for the government of Scotland and Wales and who are proud also of their British nationality.[1]

A research study by the Commission found feelings of regional identity in the regions of England also, but it is the strength of such loyalties – compared with class, for example – that is the important issue. Three surveys of Scottish opinion in the last decade – one before the Nationalists' electoral success – demonstrate how strongly and consistently Scots people consider themselves Scottish before they consider themselves British. In two Glasgow studies of 1965 and 1970 more than three quarters of people 'thought of themselves' as part of a national grouping which was not British. In 1973–74 another study found similar results: 67.5 per cent of respondents preferred to consider themselves Scottish rather than British. When people in Glasgow in 1965 were asked whether they felt they had more in common with Scots of a different class to themselves or with English people of their own class, 56 per cent chose other Scots and only 19 per cent chose English of their own class. In a direct choice they appeared to consider nationality of more importance than class.

In Scotland, nine out of ten residents are also Scots born – indeed Scotland is the most homogenous of all the 'regions' of Britain in this respect. It could not be expected that a sense of Welsh identity would be as widespread. A Strathclyde University study of the late 1960s found that 69 per cent of people in Wales considered themselves Welsh. While they found that the higher people were up the social scale the less frequently they considered themselves to be Welsh before British, the investigators also found that at least 55 per cent of those interviewed in every social group and region of Wales considered themselves Welsh – as opposed to British or English.

Table 1. How people see their national identity in Wales and Scotland (%)[2]

National identity	Wales	Scotland
Welsh	69	1
British	15	29
English	13	0
Scottish	1	67
Others/don't know	1	4

II

As far as Wales is concerned, the nationalism of the people owes very little to nineteenth- or twentieth-century institutions of government. 'For Wales read England' wrote the *Encyclopaedia Britannica*, emphasising the fact that Wales has not recently enjoyed life as an independent political entity. It has not had an administrative system of its own, nor has it had its own legislature despite one or two short-lived attempts to create one in the Middle Ages. Until modern times it did not have a recognised capital city (many in fact regarded Liverpool – not Cardiff – as its centre) and until 1893 there was no Welsh University. Even the English-Welsh frontier has remained ambiguous. The English language became the official language from 1536 onwards.

The integration of Wales and England was achieved before the growth of a centralising monarchy or a centralised state and it probably owed less to the conquests of Edward I than to the peaceful assimilation achieved under the Welsh Tudors. It was enacted unilaterally in 1536 that Wales was 'to stand and continue for ever henceforth incorporated united and annexed to and with' the realm of England. Under the Acts of Union from 1536 to 1542, the English system of law and administration was extended to Wales, although a separate system of Welsh courts – the Courts of Great Session – remained in existence until 1830, and counties and shires were created in the merger which were to send representatives to Westminster.

From its incorporation until the last century, Wales had few institutions through which its identity might be expressed. Only in the last century has the practice of referring to England and Wales rather than England alone in Acts of Parliament grown up. It was in 1881 that the first Act to treat Wales separately was passed. It was not until the 1940s that a full Parliamentary day exclusively devoted to Welsh affairs was allowed. It was not until 1967 that it was officially recognised that references to 'English' in law did not automatically include Wales also. But even then the only Acts exclusively relating to Wales which were passed between 1945 and 1970 were concerned with the Welsh language and Welsh cultural institutions.

Although the writer D. J. Williams suggested that 'Wales has no history apart from strikes, split chapels, a rugby team and a handful of short winded boxers', Lloyd George said that no one could read the history of Wales for ten minutes without realising its distinctiveness. This identity has been maintained over time through the Welsh language and religion. Language is usually taken to identify differing nationalities. While English became the official language of Wales in the sixteenth century – and perhaps before that – the Tudors allowed the translation of the Bible into Welsh, thereby encouraging the continuance of Welsh speaking. In 1870, when the Education Act prescribed English as the sole medium of instruction in Welsh schools, 25 per cent of the population still spoke only Welsh. But the decline of the Welsh-speaking population has been pronounced over the last century. While more than half of Welsh people spoke the language at the beginning of the twentieth century, now fewer than a quarter do. In South Wales only 13 per cent speak Welsh fluently. And in the country as a whole only 13 per cent of those under 30 speak Welsh.

If language was important so too were the Welsh religious traditions from the nineteenth century. While the Scots created their own Church during the Reformation, the Reformation was accepted with little opposition in Wales. It was only after the Welsh Methodists broke with the Anglican Church in 1811 and forged a peculiarly Welsh type of nonconformity that a separate tradition was formed. By the 1850s Nonconformists outnumbered Anglicans. In 1904 there were five Nonconformists for every two Anglicans and in 1920 it was finally accepted that the Anglican Church in Wales should be disestablished. In 1968 45 per cent of Welsh people identified themselves as Nonconformists. The use of the Welsh language in religion is the most important reason why Welsh has survived. It was, as the Hughes-Parry Committee on the Welsh language of 1967 remarked, 'the principal reason why Welsh held its ground so successfully in contrast to the much swifter decay of languages like Irish, Gaelic or Cornish'. In 1968, for example, 72 per cent of Welsh speakers were of the Nonconformist religion.

A sense of Welshness was fostered also by external pressures: its strength grew as the distinctiveness of Wales was threatened. Thus, much of the impulse for home rule from the 1870s onwards was religious – a desire for Sunday closing and for temperance reform, a demand for the disestablishment of the Anglican Church in Wales, and a reaction to the Education Act of 1870. But, in the absence of other institutions capable of maintaining the vigour of a Welsh nationality, the culture of Wales came to be increasingly threatened by the decline of religious observance and the growth of British and international communications. The problem for Welsh nationalists is that the old symbols of national identity – language and religion – are no longer so potent. Thus the Welsh National Party – Plaid Cymru – has continually to recreate a sense of Welshness. As the President of Plaid Cymru said in 1968, 'We are not just being denied self-expression as a nation today . . . we are fighting in the last ditch for our very identity.'

Unlike Wales, Scotland had a centralised administrative and legislative system before its Union with England in 1707. However corrupt and inefficient, and however much it was the tool of either royal government or nobles, a Scottish Parliament existed in the seventeenth century. Since the Reformation, a distinctive Church of the collegial Presbyterian rather than hierarchical Episcopal type had existed and survived in Scotland in the face of many attempts to over-turn it. Unlike Wales, Scotland had its own universities and a fully developed legal system. But despite occasional popular interventions in the wars of independence between Scotland and England and the Reformation prior to the eighteenth century, it is indisputable that in 1707 Scotland was run by an oligarchy. Scotland had a state before it was a nation. Even in 1832, there were only 4,500 electors in a Scotland which, it was commonly said, was no more than 'one rotten borough'.

However, the continued existence and independence after 1707 of Scotland's social institutions – her law, her religion, and her separate educational and local authority systems – was protected. Indeed, while the Act of Union stated that 'the laws which concern public right, policy and civil government throughout the whole United Kingdom' were to prevail, it also stipulated that 'no alteration be made in laws which concern private right except for the evident utility of the subjects within Scotland'. Scottish institutions could continue relatively undisturbed for the next century at least.

Unlike Wales, therefore, Scotland possessed officially recognised institutions through which its nationalism could be expressed. Amongst the most important of these were educational and legal systems which gave Edinburgh the status of a capital and adminis-trative centre and allowed for the development of a Scottish culture. It still proved necessary for the British – as they soon became – rulers to subdue the Highlands with force and some brutality. Notable examples are the reaction to the Jacobite risings in 1715 and 1745 and the terrible depopulation of the Highlands in the nineteenth century (so that the land could be used to raise sheep and support shooting estates for their wealthy London based owners). The memory of these events still lingers in the romantic recollection of many Scots who have never lived in the Highlands – but the point here is that the oppression could be accomplished by the use of the old Scottish legal institutions and not by their destruction. Scottish education remained Scottish; Scotland had four universities, while England had two. Even in 1868, one Scot in every 140 attended a secondary school and one in every 1,000 a university; this contrasted favourably with one in every 1,300 in England. In Scotland, as in Wales where the idea of 'Jacob's ladder' was popularised by the radical Tom Ellis, education was built around equality of opportunity, or 'the democratic intellect'. This implied that no able child, irrespective of his background, should be deprived in education. As recently as 1920, one in every four of British university graduates came from a Scottish university.

But, as in nineteenth-century Wales, Scotland's churches were the most important distinguishing feature of her national life. With the adoption of a Presbyterian rather than an Episcopalian form of religious organisation went the stronger position of the Roman Catholic Church. The Catholic faith had survived in the Highlands and in a few other remote rural pockets and after the large Irish immigrations of the nineteenth and early twentieth centuries it grew in numbers and vigour. In 1896 there were more than a million members of the Presbyterian churches and a third of a million Roman Catholics in Scotland: there were fewer than 30,000 Episcopalians. By 1966, the Church of Scotland had more than one-and-a-quarter million formal members and the Roman Catholics claimed 800,000 adherents: there were no more than 54,000 practising an Anglican religion. In addition, sport developed separately in both Scotland and Wales.

Until 1914, the Church was a more powerful social influence than government. Government's presence in most areas was restricted to the police and the post office. In Wales there were few social institutions through which national identity could be expressed and fostered. Thus there was never a sufficiently vigorous sense of national identity to galvanise a secessionist faction. In Scotland, however, there was no shortage of social institutions which were distinctively Scottish. But feelings of national identity were expressed politically only in rare instances throughout the first two hundred years of the Union. As in Wales, this was largely a product of industrialisation: not only was there little state involvement in the process of economic transformation but the frustrated aspirations by which nationalism was fuelled in other countries were, to a great extent, absorbed by the opportunities offered Scots in the expanding Empire. In Scotland, then, nationalism became at once widespread and safely non-political. Because it was non-political and focused on cultural, religious, and recreational aspects of life, Scottish nationalism was, for a long time, no threat to the establishment and many establishment figures felt free to cultivate nationalism. When the Prince of Wales (George IV to be) was ordered to tour the Highlands by Melbourne's Cabinet and to wear the kilt there, it was 1820 and the memory of the Jacobite rebellion was still fresh in the mind. But things changed so rapidly thereafter that it was possible for Queen Victoria to visit Balmoral in 1848 and buy it in 1852. There was no threat to the union in the monarch owning a private retreat in northern Scotland nor in her being accompanied by a bekilted Scotsman, John Brown. On the contrary, the adoption of the symbols of Scottish nationalism and

Welsh nationalism by the monarchy showed how domesticated these eccentric costumes had become.

III

Home rule movements in both Scotland and Wales have their roots in the 1880s. These movements have tried – with some success – to turn the widespread sense of nationality in Scotland and Wales to their own use – just as, the Labour Party tried to turn the widespread sense of working class solidarity to its own use at about the same time. But just as someone may identify himself as working class without voting Labour, many proud Scots and Welshmen have nothing to do with the National parties or the home rule movements of their countries. (We shall distinguish between nationalism as a sentiment and the National parties by capitalising the latter.)

In Scotland the pressures which brought the establishment of the Scottish Home Rule Association in 1891, had first been directed towards the re-establishment of the office of Scottish Secretary. In Wales, Cymru Fydd – founded in 1886 – was a Liberal pressure group whose primary objective was the disestablishment of the Church of England. It was not until the 1920s that Nationalist parties – competing in elections – were finally constituted.

It was the disenchantment of home rulers with the promise as well as the performance of the established parties that fostered the first Nationalist parties. In 1925 Plaid Cymru was formed specifically 'to keep Wales Welsh-speaking'. It abjured any precise commitment to home rule or to independence. The party fought one seat in the 1929 general election, and two in 1931. It was only in 1930 that the party registered its commitment to self-government and to Welsh representation at the League of Nations.

The Scottish Home Rule Association suffered from disputes between its radical and moderate factions. This led ILP member John MacCormick to form the National Party of Scotland in 1928. MacCormick was convinced that the British parties would never take the cause of Scotland seriously. The National Party's policy was 'self-government for Scotland with independent status within the British group of nations'. The National Party coexisted in Scotland with the extreme separatist group the Scots National League. This became the Scottish Party in 1932. The Scottish Party was rather more cultural than political in its orientation and had members with both left- and right-wing political views. The two groups merged in 1934 to form the Scottish National Party (SNP) in which the moderate elements prevailed.

MacCormick's description shows how moderate the new party's aims were:

The establishment in Scotland of a Parliament which shall be the final authority on all Scottish affairs including taxation and finance. Both parties are agreed that the institution of tariff barriers between Scotland and England is undesirable and that imperial matters, defence and foreign policy should remain matters of joint concern between Scotland and England[4]

In 1934 the SNP's constitution stated modestly:

The object of the party is self government for Scotland on a basis which will enable Scotland as a partner in the British empire to develop its national life to the fullest advantage.[5]

The effective control of the party until the Second World War remained in the hand of the moderate rather than the separatist wing. Its secretary, MacCormick, hoped for a pact between the major parties – there was an agreement between Labour and the SNP in the Greenock by-election in 1937 – to secure a measure of home rule. The relationship between the SNP and the other parties was helped by the fact that SNP members were not barred from membership of other parties.

In Wales the emphasis of Plaid Cymru had been cultural and linguistic from the outset. This suited a nation whose major national institutions were cultural. But in Scotland, where, significantly, there was a tradition of separate administration, the SNP quickly suppressed its cultural wing. The SNP cut itself off from the sort of literary revivalism which was the mainspring of Plaid in Wales. The best known Scottish poet Hugh MacDiarmid, also a communist of a kind, did not stay in the SNP, nor was he encouraged to. For all his strong nationalism he wrote scathingly of the direction the SNP took under MacCormick's leadership. He was later to castigate the SNP for exhibiting 'No concern with things of fundamental importance, with the great spiritual issues underlying the mere statistics of trade and industry'. As he put it in 1968:

I could never be bothered wi' MacCormick. He believed in practical politics and had no time for awkward culture. Art and culture means everything to Scotland. Practical politics, as every Scot knows, are rubbish.[6]

The feeling was mutual. MacCormick described MacDiarmid as 'politically one of the greatest handicaps with which any national movement could have been burdened'.[7]

In Wales it was precisely those counterparts to MacDiarmid who sought a national language as the medium for cultural and social revival who dominated Plaid Cymru. So paramount was the need to create and foster a sense of Welshness that Plaid played down social and economic issues. The moving spirit of the party, Saunders Lewis, had set the tone in 1926:

What then is our nationalism? This: a return to the medieval principle; a denial of the benefits of political uniformity and a demonstration of its ill effects, thereby arguing in favour of the principle of unity and variety. Not a fight for Wales' independence but for Wales' civilisation.

First of all, let us not ask for independence for Wales, not because it is impracticable but because it is not worth having. .... It is materialistic and cruel, leading to violence, oppression, and ideas already proved to be bad. .... So let us insist on having not independence but freedom.[8]

In 1932, when self-government first became a Plaid Cymru objective, the emphasis remained on the need 'to safeguard the culture, language, traditions and economic life of Wales'. Plaid Cymru was thus isolated from the economic discontents of the Welsh people between the wars. In 1937, just as South Wales had been recognised as a depressed area needing special government economic aid, a leading Nationalist, Professor J. F. Daniel, wrote:

It is in the poetry of Taliesen and Dafydd Namor, in the ruling conceptions of the ancient laws of Wales far more than in the Special Areas Acts of five year programmes, that the salvation of the Welsh is to be found.[9]

This emphasis has remained. In the 1959 election Plaid's programme asserted its first aim was 'to awaken the national Welshness of the Welsh people'. Even more recently, in 1970, Gwynfor Evans, Plaid's first member of Parliament, could make the same point when he said, 'We prefer to talk of freedom than of independence.'

Paradoxically, the Welsh National Party, which does not take social and economic issues as seriously as the SNP, is united on these issues: it is a social democratic party and competes with the Labour Party in Wales for the votes of working-class people. The SNP, on the other hand, is torn between Social Democrats and Reactionaries. From 1962 to 1979 the SNP was led by Mr William Wolfe, certainly the nicest man to lead a serious political organisation in Britain. Wolfe was a very hard-working chairman who could not be attacked by any member of the party. He also did much to reinforce the loyalty of the party's active supporters by virtue of an extraordinary memory for names and faces. Precisely because he had no clear position on social issues he was well suited to holding his socially diverse party together. His successor is Gordon Wilson (MP for Dundee East). Wilson is a much harder man and though not an extremist on social issues he is unacceptable to the social democrats because he refuses to acknowledge the existence of class problems. The SNP's parliamentary leader since 1970 has been the avuncular Donald Stewart (MP for the Western Isles), but though he too is thought to be right of centre, the leaning is not pronounced.

The social democratic wing of the SNP believe that the Scots basically lean to the left and that the SNP must shatter the Labour Party's hold on the unions and on working-class voters in and around Glasgow if it is ever to make a real breakthrough to majority power. Among the most prominent members of the group have been Margo MacDonald, one-time MP for Govan and Senior Vice-President; Stephen Maxwell, a great asset to the party when he was their full-time press officer; and John MacCormick's two sons, Ian – former MP for Argyll – and Neil, Professor of Public Law at Edinburgh University, who is the party's chief constitutional thinker. Another important member is George Reid, former MP for Stirling East and Clackmannan.

The right of the party is led by Douglas Crawford, former MP for Perth and East Perthshire, an economic consultant who is not ashamed of his financial success. He is supported by Hamish Watt, a former Tory and one time MP for Banffshire. Mr Douglas Henderson, former MP for East Aberdeenshire, discomfited the leadership with an uncompromisingly populist speech at the party's conference in 1977. Mrs Winifred Ewing, who has an ILP background, and was once on the left of the party and for a time MP for Hamilton and then for Moray and Nairn, is a solicitor. The right of the party is also bullied into line by former Edinburgh *Scotsman* leader writer and now Glasgow *Sunday Mail* columnist Colin Bell. Mr Bell is also a Vice-Chairman of the party.

On the whole the social democrats in the SNP are devolutionists and were anxious during the 1974–79 Parliament to do nothing which would make it more difficult for the government to get its Bill made law. The right of the party tended to take a harder line on the constitutional question. They saw some advantage to their party in the Government's failure to deliver devolution. They also relished the prospect – which was fulfilled – of the Government's having to refuse to implement its proposals after the Scottish people had voted by a majority for them. Most of the SNP leaders support the social and economic policies which are closest to their own background. But, as we have seen in the case of Mrs Ewing, this is not always so. Neither is it always the case that the SNP leaders tend to back policies which they think will be acceptable to voters in their seats (i.e. that those who sit or stand for former Tory seats are on the right) but this is a fair rule of thumb.

It is only fair to state that SNP leaders don't like to think of themselves as on the right or the left and that their reticence is understandable: people who feel strongly about social and class issues are not inclined to join the SNP. On the contrary, those who nail their colours to the Nationalist mast are precisely those who feel their nationalism to be more important than their class. English readers may miss the flavour of this choice. Scotland (and the same is true for Wales) is a more class-divided society than England. The old class warfare stereotypes which English politicians of both Labour and Conservative parties have been trying to forget since the late 1950s apply very well in Scotland. The Conservative Party in Scotland is more Tory and the Labour Party more socialist than elsewhere. There is less middle ground between them and party preference has rarely, therefore, been a matter of choice or decision. More often it was a matter of tribal loyalty. The National Party's determination to avoid association with either side in this old game marks them off sharply from their competitors.

The National parties of Scotland and Wales differ from each other in ways which reflect the distinctiveness of their two countries. They are not only different from the British parties but also different from each other. In their attempts to turn the national consciousness of their peoples into electoral assets, each is much concerned with the differences between the interests of its people and those of England. But the rise of the National parties in the late 1960s cannot be explained by reference to their own efforts alone. Nor can they be seen simply as the beneficiaries of Scottish and Welsh citizens' unhappiness with the performance of the economy – for the economies of the two countries had performed badly in the inter-war years without the National parties benefitting. Rather, we must seek the answer in a conjunction of forces, of which the National parties' growth was one, the failure of the British economy another, the enhanced involvement of central government in the lives of ordinary citizens a third and the increased willingness of the British government to administer its policies in Scotland and Wales from Edinburgh and Cardiff a fourth. Finally, it should be noted that the Nationalist parties of Britain gained strength when many governments around the world – in Canada, France, Spain and Belgium – were being threatened by similar movements. The forces operating in Britain were operating elsewhere too.

REFERENCES

1. *Royal Commission on the Constitution, 1968–73*, Cmnd. 5460 (London: HMSO, 1973), para. 327 (referred to as 'Kilbrandon').
2. ROSE, R. *The United Kingdom as a Multi-Party State*, (Glasgow: Strathclyde University, 1970).
3. HUGHES-PARRY, D. *The Legal Status of the Welsh Language*, Cmnd. 2785 (London: HMSO, 1964–5), Vol. 23 p. 12.
4. MACCORMICK, J. *A Flag in the Wind* (London: Gollancz, 1955), p. 35.
5. Constitution of the SNP.
6. *Sunday Telegraph*, 9 Feb. 1968, cited in McLean, I: 'The rise and fall of the SNP', *Political Studies*, 18, 1970
7. MacCormick, J. *Op. cit.*, p. 35.
8. LEWIS, SAUNDERS *Principles of Nationalism*, (1926) first English edition Plaid Cymru, 1965.
9. DANIEL, J. F. *Welsh Nationalism: What it Stands for*, (London: Fayler Welsh Co., 1937), p. 40.

Chapter two

THE GROWTH OF GOVERNMENT AND ADMINISTRATION IN SCOTLAND AND WALES

I

The history of the last century is, to a large extent, the story of growing government intervention in the economy and in the everyday lives of citizens. Government has moved to the centre of the social and economic life of the country. The extent of the shift can be illustrated by the growth in the number of civil servants. In 1870 there were 50,000 British civil servants; in 1970 there were more than half a million. The growth in the importance of government in the lives of citizens can also be illustrated by the change in the number of people who earn their livelihood in the public sector (such as school teachers, social workers, train drivers, miners, policemen and civil servants). In 1870 fewer than one wage-earner in ten owed their employment to government: now one in four does. This is a total of more than 5 million people. Another measure of the increased economic importance of governmental activity is the increased proportion of the nation's annual product which government spends: whereas in 1870 this amounted to 9 per cent of the Gross Domestic Product (GDP), a century later the figure was nearly half. A further measure of the economic power of government is the proportion of people whose main source of income is a state allowance – for example pensioners, students and those on social security and unemployment benefit.

British government has certainly grown, but it is not so clear that it has changed. Neither is it clear that for all its growth it satisfies the economic aspirations of the British people or successfully resolves economic or social conflict. On the contrary, much recent discontent with British government has focused on government's failure in just these respects. And yet, until Mr Heath took Britain into the Common Market – partly as a way of trying to jolt the country out of its economic torpor – and the devolution argument gained headway, the old habits of government which had served in a quieter time still prevailed. During the First World War, when the Government was concerned with how its recently enlarged functions should be organised, it appointed a Royal Commission under Lord Haldane to look into the matter. This reported in favour of administration by function: Ministries should be organised 'on the basis of the service performed' rather than 'the persons dealt with'. In other words, government should have Ministries of Health and Education as well as Defence and Foreign Affairs, and not Ministries for Scotland, Wales, Northern Ireland, East Anglia and London.

It is ironical that almost contemporaneously with the Haldane Report a Speaker's Conference (that is, a parliamentary committee) on government by regional area came to the opposite conclusion. This Conference, which had been set up in an attempt to deal mainly with the Irish problem, recommended the creation of several legislatures (to be called 'Councils'). The Conference's ideas were similar to the recent devolution proposals. But by the time the Conference reported, the Irish were no longer interested in remaining part of the UK and the Liberal Party, which had been sympathetic to the idea of 'Home Rule all around', was rapidly losing ground. Thus, for a long while, the ideas of the Haldane Commissioners predominated.

II

At the time of this disagreement between the Haldane Commission and the Speaker's Conference, Scotland was relatively well placed to develop its own administrative institutions. Wales was not. There was not to be a Welsh Office until 1964, but the office of Scottish Secretary had been created in 1885. This became the one government department within the United Kingdom based on 'the persons dealt with' rather than 'the function performed'. Even Northern Ireland did not have its own Ministry – it was the responsibility, until the present troubles, of the Home Office.

In its early decades this Scottish Secretary and his department were of little import, but as we shall see, they grew. The Scottish Office now performs many government functions in Scotland. Most of its staff work in Edinburgh and all are responsible, through a team of junior ministers, to the Secretary of State for Scotland, a Minister with a seat in the British Cabinet. This is a system – it is in principle similar to one operated in Wales – which is known as 'administrative devolution'. The Government's civil servants who deal with many public functions in Scotland are grouped together under a single ministerial team. They should, therefore, be able to co-ordinate the operations of government in Scotland better than the large number of departments dealing with English affairs. They should also be able to take the special legal, social and economic features of Scotland into account when administering the law and to be rather closer to the Scottish people than if the Scottish Office did not exist. Nevertheless 'administrative devolution' of this kind does give rise to some tensions.

The political masters of the Scottish Office are physically removed from their civil servants. The politicians need to be in Westminster much of the time, and, more important, the political colour of the Scottish Office's ministerial team reflects the balance of power within the British parliament, not the balance of power within Scotland. When, for example, there was a Conservative Government in Britain from 1970 to 1974, the Scottish and Welsh Offices' teams were composed of Conservative MPs and Peers even though Scotland and Wales had elected a majority of Labour MPs. This anomaly did not go unnoticed in Scotland or Wales. But it was nearly a century after the office of Scottish Secretary had been created that the pressure developed.

Until the First World War, Scottish business was transacted primarily by Statutory Boards, which were not directly responsible to Parliament and kept themselves at arm's length from the Scottish Office (which operated from Dover House in Whitehall). These Boards were responsible for domestic policy matters such as the poor law, public health, fisheries and law and order. As the Gilmour Committee remarked:

The chief reasons for the prevalence of Boards are, we think, historical. The system took root when there was no Secretary of State and its growth was no doubt partially due to the difficulty of administering a country four hundred miles away from the seat of government and the consequent difficulty of operating the ordinary type of Parliamentary-Ministerial administration...'[1]

Despite rationalisation of the Board system after the First World War – the Board of Health created in 1919 took over all central government's responsibility for the functions of the local government, poor relief, national insurance and health boards – the system came under increasing criticism because full ministerial responsibility was lacking. In 1926, in fulfilment of a Government promise of 1921, the Scottish Secretary was upgraded to Secretary of State and the holder was given a seat in the British Cabinet. Under the Registration of Offices (Scotland) Act of 1928, three Departments, Health, Agriculture and Prisons, were created which would 'act under the control and direction' of the Secretary of State. Shortly after this, the first Secretary of State, Sir John Gilmour, was appointed Chairman of a Parliamentary committee which was asked to 'enquire and report on the duties of the Scottish Office'. The Gilmour Committee concluded that while 'since 1885 and especially in the last decade the scale of his (the Secretary of State's) responsibility in nearly all these fields has increased enormously', the pattern of domestic administration reflected a 'picture of considerable diversity and haphazard growth revealing no underlying or consistent principle'. There were, they stated, anomalies which called for correction.

The Gilmour Committee decided not to pursue an enquiry into the whole government of Scotland, but restricted themselves to reviewing the general relationship existing between the various parts of the machinery of Scottish administration – so far as it was under the control of the Secretary of State. But their recommendations were far-reaching. Although they did not accept the view 'which would solidify the whole administration of Scotland into one imposing pyramid with a supreme administrative head', they recommended that the Scottish Office should be transferred to Edinburgh to incorporate responsibility for the Prisons Department and most of the remaining Boards: that a Scottish Education Department be created and that the Secretary of State should be responsible for the work of four departments whose permanent heads would 'be responsible to the Secretary of State for advising him thereon as and when necessary'. These recommendations were accepted and a new home for the Scottish Office, St Andrew's House, built on a prominent site in central Edinburgh, was opened in 1939.

Additional responsibilities were transferred to the Scottish Office during the Second World War and after. The Secretary of State for Scotland acquired responsibility for forestry, town and country planning, fishing, crown lands and civil defence, and, in line with the recommendations of the Gilmour Committee, these functions were organised within the Scottish Office on a functional basis within the four departments – Agriculture, Health, Home and Education. Further rationalisation occurred following the report of the Royal Commission on Scottish Administration chaired by Lord Balfour (1954), when highways, animal health, and responsibility for justices of the peace were added.

While the Balfour's Committee's recommendations for administrative devolution to the Scottish Office were conservative, their report did pave the way for the addition of further powers at a later stage. Balfour was mainly concerned with the activities of British and

United Kingdom Departments in Scotland. His report concluded:

Scottish controllers (of UK ministries) should have an opportunity of expressing the Scottish point of view when policy is being formulated at departmental Headquarters and should also be in a position to expound new policy clearly and properly.[2]

It was those areas of British administration in Scotland – trade and industry, transport and economic planning – to which Balfour referred which were to be devolved in the 1960s and 1970s. In 1962 a Scottish Development Department was formed within the Scottish Office to handle some of these responsibilities, and in 1973 they had grown so much that a fifth major department was established, the Scottish Economic Planning Department. Further devolution of administrative responsibility then became unlikely until the result of the government's effort to enact a bill giving effect to 'legislative and executive devolution' was clear.

Much as the administrative remit of the Scottish Office has expanded, political control over it has never been a settled matter. In 1919 a Parliamentary Under-Secretary for Health was added; this post was upgraded in 1926 to Parliamentary Under-Secretary of State for Scotland. Two more such posts were created, one in 1940 and another in 1952. In 1951 a post of Minister of State for Scotland was created – some Governments have had two such posts, one of whom is usually a peer. But at the same time as the political control over Scottish Office functions was growing the Government was creating more ad hoc Boards of the type the Scottish Office was meant to replace. Some of these Boards – such as the Scottish Development Agency and the Highlands and Islands Development Board – were the responsibility of the Scottish Office, as we have seen, but others – such as the Scottish Arts Council – were not. Some were responsible to more than one ministry. No Government has had a settled policy on giving new responsibilities to the Scottish Office or to appointed Boards, and it is far from clear why some of the latter were created. But there is no doubt that the creation of ad hoc Boards run by appointed members has diluted democratic control over the functions of government in Scotland, giving rise to demands for greater democratic accountability.

For all the increased power of the Scottish Office – with its elaborate structure of departments and boards – the key political questions about it must be: does government in Scotland differ from the administration of the same functions in England? If not, does administrative devolution amount to anything other than a Westminster housekeeping procedure? If the Scottish Office is different, is it different because it is more Scottish, or more (or less) efficient? There are no clear answers. It is clear that the Scottish Office does not slavishly follow changes made for England by the Whitehall ministries. Sometimes the difference is a matter of political judgement. Scotland is thought unready for a reform accepted in England. Divorce law was reformed in England and Wales long before it was reformed in Scotland. Homosexual acts between consenting adults, now legal in England and Wales, are not legal in Scotland. But sometimes Scotland precedes England in making a change. Social work services were reformed first. And the Scottish system for dealing with children who are in trouble (either with the law or with their parents or school) was more thoroughly reformed at the end of the 1960s and some would say is now more advanced than the English system. Social reforms in the two countries are rarely the same, because laws, customs, and religious backgrounds are different. On the other hand, while there are differences, Scotland is more like England than either country is like France or Ireland.

III

Scotland's administration was twice scrutinised by official committees before the Commission on the Constitution was appointed in 1968. No committee examined the state of Welsh administrative life before that date. The nearest Wales came to such an examination was in the annual reports of the Council of Wales which in the 1950s became a major pressure group for the setting up of a separate Welsh Office. The growth of regional administration in Wales had been more akin to the development of regional outposts for the major departments of state in the rest of the United Kingdom – a process speeded up by the decentralisation occasioned by war. There had been no tradition of a separate Welsh administration since the growth of the centralised state. Hence it was argued that the problems of Wales were not unique or that Wales was neither large nor uniform enough to constitute a unit of administration. It was not until 1944 that there was a day's debate in the House of Commons exclusively concerned with the future of Wales. Neville Chamberlain summed up the establishment view best when he compared Wales to Scotland:

The two cases are not parallel, for Scotland always had different systems of law and administration from those in England ... Wales on the other hand since Henry VIII's Act of 1536 has been closely incorporated with England and there has not been and is not now any distinct law or administrative system calling for the attention of a separate Minister.[3]

The same forces, however, were at work in Wales. Administrative differentiation by region led to the demand for regional decentralisation and eventually to the demand for democratic control of the regional administration. Education, the focus of controversy in the 1870s, led the way. After the 1870 Education Act, which prescribed English as the language of instruction in the schools when 25 per cent of the population spoke Welsh, the process started. The Welsh Intermediate Act of 1889 led to the Central Wales Board of Education of 1896 and the Welsh Department of the Board of Education – the first Welsh Division of a central department – in 1907. A. T. Davies, the Permanent Secretary of the new department, remarked prophetically: '. . . the most important service the establishment of a Welsh department has rendered to Wales is undoubtedly a recognition accorded to the fact of the separate and distinct identity of Wales'.[4]

A Welsh Department of the Ministry of Agriculture was set up in 1911. Six separate departments for Welsh affairs within British central government ministries were created between 1900 and 1913. The Second World War accelerated regional decentralisation in the United Kingdom. By 1945 there were fifteen government departments with Welsh sections. It is of some significance for future developments that the geographical sections of these ministries did not cater for units smaller than the nation. Thus the decision of Labour Ministers (both Welshmen as it happened) to reject that notion of creating separate health and social service administrations for North and South Wales was important.

With the creation of a nominated body, the Advisory Council for Wales and Monmouthshire, in 1949 Wales was accorded its first semi-official voice. It was to be 'the channel between the needs of the Welsh people and the Government'. The subsequent pressures generated by this were to be important. Its constant refrain was that 'far too little co-ordination of the activities of the departments operating in Wales' was taking place and that the regional arms of government were incapable of 'decisive action to deal with Welsh problems, being vested with little real independence or power of decision'. This was the chorus which led to the establishment of a Welsh Office parallel to the Scottish Office.

The demands for the establishment of a Welsh Office eventually became, in the view of the first Parliamentary Under-Secretary (and erstwhile opponent of devolution), Ted Rowlands, 'irresistible'. Before this the Conservative Governments of the 1950s, while attempting to resist, had accepted a Welsh day in Parliament, an annual White Paper on government action in Wales, a quarterly conference of heads of Welsh departments, a Ministry of Welsh Affairs attached to the Home Office, and a Welsh Grand Committee (1960). The creation of the Welsh Office – a Labour election promise from 1959 – was much disputed. For Crossman it was 'an idiotic creation' and a 'completely artificial new office' and in 1964 the Welsh Office began its life with only the regional branch of the Ministry of Transport within its ambit. As Randall recorded,

It took nearly five years for the Secretary of State to assume full executive responsibility for health in Wales. The explanation for the delay lies chiefly in the jealous guardianship exercised by Whitehall departments over the principle of centralised administration.

But while pressure for the creation of the post of Secretary of State had come from outside government, after 1964, as Rowlands recorded.

The new office and the Secretary of State became a focus for pressure for further devolution from within. But the process by which he was created derived little from any Whitehall adherence to a concept of national administration and political decentralisation, and more from ad hoc adjustments and compromises extracted from the system by political pressures and manoeuvres.[5]

In 1964 the Welsh Office spent £48,000. By 1974 it was £1,170m with responsibilities in Wales for the functions exercised by ministries in England. The devolution of education, roads, health and later industrial and agricultural powers to the Welsh Office followed the initial transfer of power.

IV

There were limits to the extent of administrative devolution in Scotland and Wales. While in 1954 the Balfour Commission stated for Scotland that 'in the absence of convincing evidence to the contrary the machinery of government should be designed to dispose of Scottish business in Scotland', and that British departments in Scotland should make suitable arrangements to transact Scottish affairs, it argued further that any proposal to divide ministerial functions on a geographical basis rather than on a functional basis:

would require to be supported by clear evidence that (a) distinctive Scottish interests would be better served, and (b) the interests which Scotland has in common with the rest of the UK would not suffer.[6]

This definition narrowed the scope for devolution in Balfour's recommendations to central government relationships with local authorities, the legal system and matters arising from distinctive Scottish conditions and was a recipe for conservatism – and pragmatism.

But the essential fact was that the assumption of their new responsibilities by the Welsh and Scottish Offices gave Scotland and Wales an established political dimension – the focus for pressure groups and political argument – for the first time since their incorporation into the United Kingdom. More than that, the assumption grew that the Scottish and Welsh Secretaries were in fact Scotland's and Wales' ministers for a whole range of grievances outside their formal responsibilities. As early as the 1920s, Lord Birkenhead had said that the Scottish Secretary spoke not for a department, but for a country. In 1936, the Gilmour Committee, which called the office of Secretary of State 'a penumbra' concluded:

He is popularly regarded as Scotland's Minister and our evidence shows that there is an increasing tendency to appeal to him on all matters that have a Scottish aspect – even if on a strict view they are outside the province of his duties as statutorily defined . . . there is a wide and undefined area in which he is expected to be the mouthpiece of Scottish opinion in the cabinet and elsewhere.[7]

In 1953 Sir David Milne told the Balfour Commission that the Secretary of State was 'Scotland's Minister, . . . concerned in all matters affecting the social and economic life of the country and the presentation of Scottish needs to government'. The conclusions of the Balfour Committee went further:

He is in a very unique position in that advised by such representative organisations as the Scottish Council (Development and Industry), the Scottish Board for Industry and the Advisory Panel of the Highlands and Islands, he claims to represent an agreed Scottish viewpoint over a very wide field.[8]

Much the same happened in Wales after 1964. As the first Secretary of State James Griffiths wrote of the time, 'Everywhere I found pride in the recognition which the appointment of a Secretary of State and the establishment of the Welsh Office has brought to our nation.' Harold Wilson, the Prime Minister, informed the House of Commons in November 1964 that:

With his new wide range of powers the Secretary of State for Wales would be able to express the voice of Wales and put pressure on the Government and other Welsh Departments to see that Wales gets a fair crack of the whip.[9]

In 1973 Kilbrandon summed up the process of administrative devolution:

The main feature of the existing system of administrative devolution to Scotland and Wales is that in each country the Secretary of State has in certain subjects full responsibility both for the formulation of policy and its execution and in others a more general responsibility for representing the country's interests to departmental Ministers individually and to Ministers collectively in Cabinet.[10]

The growth of administrative devolution did not dissipate pressures for legislative control in Scotland and Wales; these pressures were, however, intermittent rather than constant from the end of the First World War. While the Liberal Party had promised Home Rule Bills for Scotland and Wales before 1914, the party was never again to be in a position to keep the promises. For the growing Labour Parties in Scotland and Wales, home rule had been an early imperative, but between the wars Labour was never in a majority in the House of Commons. After 1945 it had a majority but its concern had shifted to the needs of economic reconstruction and the control of the commanding heights of the economy. Devolution would not again be a priority for that party until the 1970s. Indeed, in Wales after 1945 the disagreements within the Labour Party were over the advisability of creating a Welsh Office at all. In 1949 the Welsh Council of Labour affirmed its support for administrative devolution to Wales. In Scotland the Labour Party, which had been in favour of devolution until 1958, never took its commitment seriously enough to work out a practical scheme. It is true that there were some attempts to bring the government's Scottish and Welsh agencies under better democratic scrutiny short of creating a devolved directly elected legislature to do the job. In 1948 the Scottish Grand Committee (a House of Commons committee consisting of all Scottish and some other MPs which takes the committee stage of all Scottish legislation) was given additional power, and in the late 1960s a separate Select Committee of the House of Commons on Scottish Affairs was set up. But it was soon abandoned along with many other new Select Committees.

However unsystematic the approach of both Conservative and Labour Governments to administrative devolution, and however little they advanced democratic control of the administratively devolved agencies, the sporadic periods of change show there was a well of sympathy within both parties for some devolution. Though neither party was serious about devolution, equally, neither was adamantly opposed. In such circumstances it was possible for internally generated administrative pressures for further specific measures of devolution to win the day from time to time without creating a fuss in public. The politics of devolution remained an insiders' game in which the devolutionists won a series of small victories which had the cumulative effect of creating a large government department – the Scottish Office – in Edinburgh and a small but obviously growing department – the Welsh Office – in Cardiff.

v

Few people cared about Whitehall's internal administrative arrangements. In both Scotland and Wales, as in England, the overriding concerns of politicians and the public were the condition of the economy and unemployment. As long as there was no discernible link between the diffuse demand for self-government and the economic condition of Scotland and Wales, the pressures for devolution or separation could never be strong enough to force themselves to the centre of the political stage. In other words, devolution and self-government were irrelevant to the central issues. On the one hand, those politicians who believed in the sanctity of the market had no time for tinkering with the constitution and disliked the prospect that a new series of constitutional arrangements might make government interference in the market-place more effective. These Conservatives and Liberals also did not like the strong Socialist traditions of the peripheral nations. Better to keep them firmly hitched to dependable, sane England. On the other side, the big battalions – and most of the intellectual heavyweights – of the Socialist movement believed in a planned economy. In essence this argument continued and survived until the mid-1960s. It was in the 1950s and early 1960s that the Labour Party took the argument against economic devolution a stage further by arguing that centralised planning was not only in the interests of the country as a whole but was specifically in the interests of the poorer peripheral nations. Only by sharing the wealth of the English South-East and Midlands could Scotland and Wales prosper. In 1958, in the process of turning its back on its own tepid commitment to devolution, the Labour Party in Scotland put this case best when it argued:

The Labour Party in Scotland today believes that Scotland's problems can best be solved by socialist planning on a UK scale. . . . Only socialist planning which will channel industry to Scotland can preserve our national vitality. For though we are a nation with a proud history of achievement, our present and future are closely linked with Britain's.[11]

At a time when economic arguments gave support to the union few in the Labour Party rallied to the cause of self-government. Their numbers swelled only when the Scottish and Welsh Offices had increased their intervention in the Scottish and Welsh economies. Then, in part because centralised economic planning had been seen not to work, and in part because the Scots and Welsh electorate was turning away from the British parties to parties which promised that self-governments would lead to increased prosperity, the British parties did begin to think seriously about self-government for Scotland and Wales.

Successive governments involved themselves with the infrastructure of the economy and with a battery of interventionist measures – grants, subsidies, loans and assistance – to foster a new partnership with industry. In Wales and Scotland regional policy was a special tool of government intervention in depressed areas. In both countries public expenditure and public employment increased faster than in Britain as a whole, especially after 1960. First, public authorities' current expenditure grew rapidly, especially on services of direct importance to economic development. Secondly, capital investment within the two countries was undertaken increasingly by government. By the late 1960s the majority of capital investment was public and, whereas most of capital investment in industry by governments before 1960 was for nationalised industries, by the early 1970s only a third was directed to them. Though the administration of the government policies designed to increase public investment in Scotland and Wales was largely in the hands of British ministries, the Scottish, and latterly the Welsh, Offices were increasingly involved.

Heedless of the political problems which their economic and administrative policies would pile up for them, successive Governments devolved economic powers to the Scottish and later to the Welsh Office. Regional policy – the instrument chosen to bring Welsh, Scottish and other 'problem' economies into line with that of Britain as a whole – had begun to emerge in the 1930s. In 1931 the Government appointed investigators into conditions in 'the specially defined' depressed areas of the North-East, Cumberland, South Wales and the Clydeside-Lanarkshire area of Scotland. In 1934 two Commissioners for depressed areas – one for England and Wales and another for Scotland under the general control of the Scottish Secretary of State – were appointed and the Special Areas Act named South Wales and the South-West of Scotland as two of the special areas requiring new industries. The appointment of a Scottish Commissioner was a *de facto* recognition of Scotland as an acceptable unit for economic action and the Special Areas Act was a signal for the Scottish Office itself to demand discretionary powers for intervention beyond the South-West, as a memorandum to the Inter Departmental Committee on Depressed Areas argued:

It is desirable that Scotland as a whole or at least homogeneous sections of the country, especially particular counties, should be the basis of treatment leaving discretion with the Secretary of State and the Commissioner.[12]

By the late 1930s not only the Scottish Office but the also Scottish Industrial Council – a semi-official body which had commissioned a report on the state of the economy – wanted greater innovation at a Scottish level. Their report favoured a Scottish Ministry of Planning – a demand taken up by the Scottish Trades Union Congress among others. The war saw the establishment of the Scottish Council on Post-War Problems and although both the Barlow Committee and then the Labour Government of 1945 favoured centralised intervention, a Scottish Economic Conference was established in 1948 and an annual review of Scottish economic affairs promised. Nationalised industries in Scotland were to be kept under review 'in order to ensure that they are properly related to Scottish needs'.

While the Balfour Commission of 1954 opposed additional economic powers for the Scottish Office, it went a long way towards accepting a Scottish dimension in the economic management of Britain. It cited as an 'essential principle' for the government of Scotland that her 'needs and points of view should be known and brought into account at all stages in the formulation and execution of policy, that is to say, when policy is being considered, when policy is decided and when policy is announced'. In recognition of this, it recommended that as far as the Boards of Trade, Transport and Civil Aviation were concerned, Ministers should be seen to be 'personally concerned in the operation of their departments in Scotland . . . and make clear the consideration which has been given to its Scottish aspects'. There should be the 'closest co-operation between the Board of Trade and the Scottish Home Department', the Commission recommended 'as regards distribution of industry'.

As it entered the 1960s, Scotland had the administrative momentum and the pressure group support to foster ever stronger instruments of state intervention in the economy at 'Scottish level'. The Scottish Council (Development and Industry) Toothill Report (1961) – a milestone in Scottish economic thinking – rejected economic devolution, which it believed was not in Scotland's best interests. But it went on to recommend an economic statistics unit and a co-ordinating department for roads and other economically useful facilities. This led to the establishment in 1962 of the Scottish Development Department as an additional major department of the Scottish Office. It did not take the civil servants in this department long to develop the habit of looking askance at the other, more traditional, sections of the Ministry. The SDD took responsibility for local government, planning, housing, roads and later passenger transport, shipping and Highland development. In so far as the Scottish Office had an economics section this was it, and increasingly economics was what government was about. In 1963, under a Conservative administration, a Central Scotland Plan was issued embodying the SDD's ideas. Then in 1965, under Labour, a Highlands and Islands Development Board – the plans for which had been generated within the civil service and presented to the incoming Labour Secretary of State, William Ross – was established under the wing of the SDD. Shortly after the Labour Party came to power its new Prime Minister, Harold Wilson – who did more than any other British leader to raise economic hopes – spelt out, for the first time, the Secretary of State's overall responsibility for economic oversight. As the Permanent Secretary at the Scottish Office, Sir Douglas Haddow, informed the Kilbrandon Commissioners, the Secretary of State is 'responsible for taking the lead in preparing plans for economic development'.

In the same year a non-executive department, the Regional Development Department, was created to co-ordinate the work of all agencies – Scotland and United Kingdom – involved in economic planning (in Scotland). By March 1965, a Scottish Economic Planning Council and Board were set up. It soon presented a Scottish Plan for the rejuvenation of Scotland's economy.

In the mid-1970s further administrative strengthening of the Scottish Office's economic powers came almost yearly. In 1973 an Economic Planning Department was created as a fifth department of the Scottish Office. In 1975 the Government created a semi-autonomous Scottish Development Agency allied to the Scottish Office which was to assist, participate in and establish industries. The year after that the Scottish Office was given the power to make discretionary grants to industries in Scotland.

Increasingly, therefore, the state was responsible for Scotland's livelihood and increasingly the state in Scotland operated from Scotland. Administrative devolution of power over the economy was as unco-ordinated as administrative devolution of power over social welfare. In 1974 the Scottish Council reported that economic devolution was 'a manifest fiction' in that 'no one body can evolve a coordinated development strategy which is based on a coherent synthesis of economic and physical considerations'. The measures of economic devolution that took place themselves created new pressures for more co-ordination and more devolution. It was not such a long step from arguing that British Governments should devise special institutions to meet Scottish needs to suggesting that Scotland needed to operate its own institutions in a separate state.

From a later start, the Welsh Office quickly came to resemble the Scottish Office in its possession of powers for economic intervention. The Welsh Secretary speedily assumed an 'oversight' role in relation to Welsh economic affairs. The Welsh plan, *Wales: The Way Ahead*, published in 1967, was geared to the new Labour Secretary's dream of 'building a new economy' in Wales. 'I decided that Wales should be treated as one unit of economic planning,' he wrote, 'with its own planning board and executive council.' Indeed, he considered going further:

I had in mind the possibility of creating a democratically elected council for Wales to which the responsibility of the Economic Council should be transferred and to which executive powers could be transferred on this all important sphere of economic planning.[13]

As the invisible hand of the market gave way to the more robust hand of state intervention, more and more Scots and Welshmen came to be economically dependent on the state. As the state took increasing responsibility for economic welfare, it had to show that it could perform convincingly in this new role. The meek nightwatchman state was seen exchanging its humble workaday uniform for the raiments of Superman. But it had to explain itself. At first, economic success provided its own justification. Subsequently, without prosperity, the problem for the British state was particularly acute, for it ruled not one nation but three. This the Balfour Commission saw clearly even in 1954:

17. Why then has discontent again become evident? It has, we think, been aggravated by needless English thoughtlessness and undue Scottish susceptibilities, but deeper than this lie some more tangible causes. First, there has been a profound change during the last forty years in the functions of government and consequently in the machinery necessary to exercise them. Until 1914 the Government intervened little in the day to day affairs of the individual. But since then its encroachment on private activities has mounted with what has seemed to be ever-increasing intensity. Restrictions arising from two world wars, steps to meet the depression and unemployment in the inter-war period, the allocation of scarce materials, the rationing of capital

investment, the need to channel production – all these have called for regulations and controls, most of which have been organised on the Great Britain basis with ultimate authority resting in London.

18. When the State's interference with the individual was insignificant, it mattered little to the Scotsman whether this came from Edinburgh or London. But when so many domestic affairs are no longer under control of the individual and so many enterprises require some form of official authorisation, he begins to wonder why orders and instructions should come to him from London, to question whether Whitehall has taken sufficient account of local conditions and to criticise not government but what he regards, however erroneously, as English government.[14]

By their own efforts at administrative devolution, governments were forging and then pointing to the link between economic intervention and devolution. At first, this link was much more apparent to small groups of civil servants, government ministers, their economic advisers and the people who ran the quasi-independent pressure groups such as the Scottish Council (Development and Industry), than to the general public. But the penny did eventually drop in the popular mind. When it did the Nationalist parties could make headway by pointing out how ineffectively the British state was serving the needs of the Scottish and Welsh economies. When William Wolfe, who was to become Chairman of the SNP, first stood in a by-election, in West Lothian in 1962, against Tam Dalyell (who was to become the most eloquent anti-devolutionist), Wolfe made great play with the failure of the British Government to protect jobs in the local shale-oil mining industry. He struck a responsive chord in the hearts of West Lothian's voters which other nationalists were to learn to pluck as well.

The momentum of administrative aggrandisement within the Scottish and, later, the Welsh Office became allied to the pressure for government to improve the performance of the economies of Scotland and Wales, and these facts worked to the advantage of the Scottish and Welsh National Parties. Thus the pressure for political control over the Scottish and Welsh Offices did not arise entirely from the nationalism of the Scottish and Welsh peoples – that nationalism has a long history which predates the present pressure for devolution – nor did it arise entirely because of the efforts of the National parties of Scotland and Wales: it arose in fair part out of attempts of Conservative and Labour governments to deal with the increased responsibilities of government and increased popular expectations in a modern country comprised of three nations. No doubt many of the people who took an active part in expanding the roles of the Scottish and Welsh Offices were patriotic

Scots and Welshmen, but this did not necessarily make them advocates of independence for their countries. It remains to be seen whether the ammunition created as a byproduct of the increasing devolution or administrative power will be used to destroy the United Kingdom. But, before we address that problem, we have to come to grips with the social and economic changes which helped to translate the latent nationalism of many Scots and Welshmen into active support for the Nationalist parties.

REFERENCES

1. SCOTTISH OFFICE, Committee on Scottish Administration. *Report* (Gilmour), Cmd. 5563 (Edinburgh: HMSO, 1937), para. 15, p. 10.

2. ROYAL COMMISSION ON SCOTTISH AFFAIRS, 1952 - 54. *Report* (Balfour), Cmd. 9212 (Edinburgh: HMSO, 1954), para. 210, p. 98, recommendation 40.

3. CHAMBERLAIN, N. quoted in J. Griffiths *Pages from Memory*, (London: Dent, 1969), p. 195.

4. RANDALL, 'Wales in the Structure of Central Government', *Public Administration*, 50, 1972, 353-72.

5. ROWLANDS, T. 'The Politics of Regional Administration', *Public Administration*, 50, 1972, 333-51.

6. Balfour, *Report*, paras. 17-18.

7. Gilmour, *Report*, p. 19.

8. Balfour, *Report*, para. 177, p. 56.

9. Griffiths, *Op. cit.*, p. 169.

10. Kilbrandon, *Report*, para. 1022, p. 309.

11. SCOTTISH COUNCIL OF THE LABOUR PARTY. *Annual Report*, 1958.

12. SCOTTISH RECORD OFFICE FILES, DD/10 169 note on the adjustment of special areas (Scotland).

13. Griffiths, *Op. cit.*, p. 170.

14. Balfour, *Report*, paras. 17, 18.

Chapter three
THE MODERNISATION OF SCOTLAND AND WALES

Gwynfor Evans, the President of Plaid Cymru, has put his finger on a most important point:

Until recently, however, Wales was not even acknowledged to be an entity for administrative and economic purposes. The progress which we have made during the last generation in this direction has given us an administration which is based for the most part on the national community and increasingly this community is the basis for economic organisation, as with the Welsh Development Agency. This is the result of long campaigning by Plaid Cymru.[1]

Administrative devolution is a great gift to the Nationalist parties because it gives official sanction to their claim that Scotland and Wales are the relevant units for economic action by government. But we may doubt whether Mr Evans is entirely accurate when he claims that Westminster has conceded so much purely at the behest of the Nationalist parties. Or rather, we may doubt whether the large number of votes garnered by the two Nationalist parties are votes for economic devolution. On the contrary, the evidence collected for the Kilbrandon Commission showed that most Scots and Welshmen did not make the connection between economic deprivation and constitutional change. Our contention, rather, is that massive changes have been occurring in Scotland and Wales which have produced a sizeable number of socially and politically displaced people. Many of these people have turned to the Nationalist parties. The Nationalist parties have used the votes thus won to create pressure for further measures of administrative devolution – and for elected assemblies to control the administrators.

The evidence, scant and inadequate as it is, suggests that as the expectations of many (particularly Scots) voters rose, more and more of them were ready to consider alternative political options. As they left their old occupations, their old homes and their old neighbours, they left their old – and often this meant their parents' – political affiliations behind them as well. In other words, our contention is that to account for the recent thrust of nationalism one has to account both for the disenchantment of large numbers of Scots and Welshmen with the old parties as well as to account for their decision to vote for the National parties.

An important facet of the Nationalist use of the failure of government economic performance is often overlooked and needs to be underlined here. The Nationalists constantly contrast the native wealth of their countries – and their peoples – with their present poverty. They attribute the difference to the mismanagement of the economy by British (i.e. foreign) governments. But the Nationalists have *not* gained the votes of those most threatened or hurt by the poor performance of the economy. They do not do well among the poorest economic classes. Neither do they do well among the most comfortable. On the contrary, the Nationalists' success, particularly in Scotland has been among those who have benefited from recent changes in the economy. There is, of course, nothing particularly Scottish or Welsh about rapid changes in the economy. The economies of most industrialised states have changed considerably since the Second World War. Students of the politics of some of these countries – including England – have occasionally noticed the weakening of identification with the old political parties which occurs along with this economic change. In England, however, when the old ties to the class parties were weakened, whether by social change or by the sheer incompetence of the main parties, there was no readily available alternative focus for identification. In Scotland and Wales there was: the nation.

The two countries have much in common. Both are peripheral, not only to the United Kingdom, but also to the 'Golden Triangle' of European economic development. In both countries the indigenous private sector of the economy has been unadventurous: in both a high proportion of the capital employed in industry is foreign-owned. Both became reliant, manifestly over-reliant, on coal mining in the nineteenth century. Their economies were dependent on heavy industry, in Wales on iron and steel production, in Scotland on those industries plus shipbuilding. In 1950 half the Welsh industrial labour force was employed in coal or metal manufacture. In Scotland just under half were in heavy engineering, shipbuilding or coal.

This reliance on heavy industry meant that in both countries relatively highly paid skilled manual workers held an important place in the social structure. In both countries the unions were overwhelmingly controlled by these groups. In both Scotland and Wales in 1960, more than one-third of male workers were in skilled trades. The other side of this was that both countries had relatively weak middle classes. Neither had a well developed administrative group. Neither was the centre of international business or finance. Neither had the concentration of technologically sophisticated consumer industries which had become such a prominent feature of the English Midlands and South-East. Nationalist movements in many countries are dominated by middle-class activists. The striking thing about Scotland and Wales was the weakness of the middle classes of those countries. In part this weakness accounts for the weakness of the national movement.

But the condition of the two countries diverged. The first fifteen years after the end of the Second World War saw the two moving in opposite directions. Scotland was one of the most depressed areas in Britain in the post-war years. Its heavy industry was run down. In Wales, on the other hand, a gradual restructuring of the economy had taken place during the Second World War. There the proportion of workers in heavy industry fell from 40 per cent to 32 per cent during the war; it rose in Scotland. Welsh industry continued to diversify throughout the remainder of the 1940s and 1950s. Scotland knew no such improvements.

Thus it is not surprising that academic studies of the Welsh economy published in the early 1960s were optimistic. In 1961 Professor Thomas wrote:

The key note of the resurgence since 1945 is a combination of government sponsored initiatives and diversification. There has been a striking technological revolution in steel production and the expansion in manufacture has been nearly twice the rate in Great Britain as a whole. Wales has shared with other regions the benefits of the Distribution of Industry Act and the strength of the economy is shown by the negligible loss through migration in contrast with Scotland and Northern Ireland.[2]

The same study spoke of 'rejuvenation, growth and structural change' in the steel industry, and claimed that this industry had 'grown fast and changed more in shape than at any time since the iron trade began to absorb the new steel-making processes in the 1860s and 1870s'. In 1963 *The Times* rashly referred to the redevelopment of South Wales as 'one of the great success stories of the past thirty years'.

The mood of Scotland could not have been more different. In the same year as Professor Thomas's report was produced for Wales, the Toothill Report was concluding that Scotland's economy was in grave trouble. Gloomily it concluded:

While industrial production rose by 13 per cent in the UK between 1954 and 1959, the rise in Scotland was 3 per cent. In Wales the expansion was roughly the same as the average for the UK ... Scotland is relatively deficient in the science based industries and in those producing consumer durable goods. More diversification is needed in order to spread the risk and to increase the representation of the more rapidly expanding types of production.[3]

The difference of mood in the early 1960s was considerable, and yet there were some similarities between the two countries.

Most important, the decline of the coal mining industry in both countries accelerated throughout the 1960s. In Scotland employment in mining fell from 92,000 in 1960 to 35,000 in 1975. In Wales the fall was from 113,000 to 42,000. For both countries the problem was more than the simple loss of employment. It was that whole communities previously reliant on coal were threatened with extinction. The threat was all the more poignant because these mining areas had been bastions of economic power within living memory. The run-down in the mining industry led to great social stress in areas such as the Rhondda Valley (where 18 per cent of voters, even in 1966, were miners) and Lanarkshire in the West of Scotland – where the industry collapsed. But in the mining areas themselves resentment at the closure of the pits was not sufficient to provoke a rejection of traditional political loyalties. It was among those who escaped that the traditional parties had the most difficulty.

The difficulty in the mining industry was not, fortunately for Wales, repeated across the entire economy: in the 1960s employment in heavy industry in Wales actually increased. In Scotland the reverse was the case. Between 1960 and 1975 employment in Scotland in shipbuilding fell by one-third, in metals and heavy engineering by one-quarter and in textiles by a half. Some long-established basic industries disappeared from Scotland altogether, linoleum and locomotive production among them. The net effect was to displace 10,000 men a year from the productive sector. It was the skilled worker who was hit most of all. Employment in the skilled trades fell by 80,000 in Scotland between 1961 and 1971. This was a larger loss than in the preceeding forty years. By 1971 an important mark was passed: in that year for the first time more skilled workers in Scotland were employed outside than inside the productive sector.

In both Wales and Scotland there was a positive corollary to the rundown of traditional industries. In both regional policy was deployed to attract new scientific and technological industries, mostly capital intensive and usually externally controlled. But whereas in Wales a new economic base was developed from the Second World

War, in Scotland a long road had to be travelled merely to catch up. Between 1945 and 1960 in Wales, immigrant firms took on 74,000 workers and added another 8,700 between 1960 and 1965. New firms originating elsewhere which settled in Wales after 1960 added an additional 13,800. Immigrant firms established since 1945 thus accounted for 31 per cent of manufacturing employment in 1968 – representing more than half of employment in the engineering and electrical industries, the vehicle, textiles and clothing and footwear industries – and firms established between 1945 and 1951 alone accounted for 21 per cent of employment (or two-thirds of new employment). In Scotland the years before 1960 were barren ones. Whereas between 1951 and 1961 only 90 new units had been opened by incoming firms, 402 were opened between 1961 and 1974, increasing employment by 81,000 and helping to offset a loss of 120,000 in Scottish based manufacturing firms. New sectors were established in car production, instrument and electrical engineering, and petrochemicals.

Table 1. Employment in selected industries in Scotland and Wales (thousands)

Industry	1950		1960		1970		1976	
	S	W	S	W	S	W	S	W
Mining	99.5	132.0	92.1	113.0	42.9	57.0	35.3	41.2
Coal only	90.9	138.0	85.8	105.3	38.4	51.9	27.8	37.9
Metal	62.6	83.0	58.3	89.6	48.3	92.2	39.1	76.5
Heavy engineering	124.0	28.0	156.4	46.2	119.0	33.5	91.7	26.5
Shipbuilding	77.0	7.0	68.8	0.6	46.0	2.7	42.3	1.3
Textiles	117.6	16.0	109.3	17.0	87.8	19.6	57.2	14.3

One unexpected result was that both economies suffered from a degree of industrial concentration unknown before the war. The prospects of individual communities and towns were determined by the activities of one or two major employers. By 1973 more than half of Scottish manufacturing workers were employed by 110 firms. In Wales the position was similar. More than that, however, control of their economies moved further away from Scotland and Wales. Fifty-nine per cent of Scottish manufacturing workers in 1973 were employed by companies based outside Scotland – and one quarter of these by American-owned companies. In Wales, most companies were based outside Wales, and the larger the company the more likely there was to be external control. Interestingly, no political party sought to stop this trend. Each pursued a strategy that would provide jobs almost at any cost, no matter where the employing company was based.

In Scotland's case the overall changes in the structure of productive industry transformed the economy. Where once there had been an almost exclusive reliance on the heavy industries, consumer goods became crucial to the economy's growth. Whereas in Wales the metal and mechanical engineering industries were still responsible for nearly two-fifths of output in 1973, in Scotland the new industries of electronics, chemicals, instrument engineering and car vehicles which had been responsible for less than 10 per cent of industrial production in 1958 were to share 25 per cent in 1972. In the electrical engineering, for example, output increased sixfold between 1960 and 1976, and the consumer industries doubled their output in these years. These changes allowed the Scottish Office to conclude in 1976 that 'Scottish industry would appear to be more dependent on consumer demand than industry in the UK – a conclusion which is far removed from the historic view of Scotland as being dominated by heavy industry'.

The coincidence of the run-down of the heavy industries, the expansion of new industries and a shift to the service sector created new social patterns in Scotland. At one and the same time the traditional backbone of the Labour movement – the skilled worker – was being broken and the stage was being set for the development of a larger self-conscious middle class no longer dominated by lairds, lawyers and Lords. The new manufacturing industries were not major employers of labour. Indeed, to have been effective in both Wales and Scotland regional policy would have had to create three times as many jobs as it did. But the service sector was a major employer of new labour. In Wales employment in the professional and scientific sectors – insurance, teaching, health and public administration – increased in the years from 1960 to 1975 at twice the rate of the 1950s, from 168,000 to 271,000 (or 7,000 yearly). In Scotland the changes were even faster. The insurance sector grew by 80 per cent, the professional and scientific sector by 50 per cent and public administration and defence by just over 50 per cent between 1960 and 1975. By 1975 these sectors were responsible for more than a third of all employment. They had grown a quarter of a million jobs. In these sectors most of the employees were in white-collar jobs. While there was large emigration of manual workers in the 1960s, 100,000 new white-collar jobs were added. 200,000 more people in Scotland were living in white-collar families in 1971 than in 1961.

Like the rest of Britain, Wales benefited from the growth of the service sector and the technological changes altering the occupational framework of productive industry. But, while the 1960s had begun with optimism in Wales, the next fifteen years saw relative stagnation. The fall in male employment – 100,000 male jobs were lost between 1965 and 1975 – was not balanced, as in Scotland's case, by an equivalent rise in women's work – only 50,000 female jobs were created in that period. By the early 1970s Wales had the smallest female employment sector of any region of Great Britain. One consequence of this small growth in female employment was that production per head of population fell behind that of the rest of Britain and household incomes did not grow as fast as in the rest of the country. Gross Domestic Product per capita, which had been higher than in Scotland and most regions of Britain in the 1950s and early 1960s, fell behind: by the early 1970s it was the lowest of any British region. In 1975, GDP per capita, which was £1,321 in England and £1,176 in Scotland, was only £1,030 in Wales. It was 5 per cent below the average for assisted regions and 25 per cent below the average for unassisted regions.

By the early 1970s Wales appeared to have been left behind by many of the changes that were benefiting the rest of Britain. Regional policies had not been very successful, and the decline of productive employment in the more prosperous areas of the south had lessened the capacity of governments to direct industry to the distressed areas. With the prospect of a run-down in the steel industry in the mid-1970s and early 1980s, the Welsh economy approached the very crisis which Scotland had confronted fifteen years before. Thus, while in Wales the social structure had not yet been radically transformed, the Scottish social structure looked very much like that of England – indeed the south of England. By the mid-1970s a stronger middle stratum was noticeable and the skilled working class had lost much of its importance.

Scotland was affected not only by social changes that were taking place throughout Britain but by the sheer speed of change in the country. A 1974 survey showed that only half of Scots identified themselves as 'working class' or 'middle class'. The young especially were beneficiaries of the process. Twice as many young people in Scotland entered white-collar jobs in 1971 as in 1961, and by 1975 one in every four white-collar jobs was filled by someone whose parents had been manual workers.

The process of change had a spatial dimension also. While the cities and industrial towns of the west of Scotland declined or stagnated, there was a rapid growth of the suburbs and new towns. Owner-occupation increased from 25 to 33 between 1960 and 1975. By 1976, for the first time for fifty years, more homes were being built in the private sector than in the public sector. This was indeed notable in a country which was further from being a property-owning democracy than any other in Western Europe and where the provision of council housing had been an ark of the political covenant since the First World War. But the same date, Scotland's six new towns had grown to house 5 per cent of its population.

These changes brought a consumer boom in Scotland. Ownership of cars, washing machines, telephones, central heating and colour televisions increased faster in Scotland – in most cases doubling from the mid-1960s onwards – than in the rest of Britain, and half of Scots families were enjoying to the full the benefits of the consumer society denied to most of them before the 1960s. There was, in short, a revolution of rising expectations in the country.

These economic changes had three political consequences. First, the increasing involvement of government in the economy encouraged people to look to government to solve their economic problems – traditionally the province of the market. Secondly, the build-up of the economic powers wielded by the Scottish and Welsh offices – and the popularisation of the idea of Scottish and Welsh economies – induced people to take Scotland and Wales as the appropriate units against which their individual prospects should be gauged. Thirdly, however, and equally important, government intervention raised more expectations than it satisfied. The Scottish and Welsh plans produced by Labour Governments in 1965 and 1967 were symptomatic of this.

Targets for growth, employment creation and the attraction of new industries were wildly optimistic. In Wales the national plan estimated that although 15,000–25,000 jobs would be lost between 1966 and 1971, an additional 15,000 jobs would be attracted by new industries. When Professor Nevin of the University College of Wales estimated that the loss would be 59,000, his figures were dismissed and he eventually resigned from the Welsh Economic Council. The actual loss of jobs was 57,000. Equally, regional policy, operated with the stick of Industrial Development Certificates and the carrot of investment incentives, grants and loans, did not create the jobs anticipated. For Wales the conclusion of one academic study was that 'whilst regional policy contributed at most 80,000 new jobs between 1960 and 1972, a full solution to the imbalance in the Welsh labour market would have required between 200,000 and 250,000 new jobs'. In Scotland the conclusion of a similar study by the Scottish Council (Development and Industry) was the same: only a third of the jobs required and promised had been created. What was required, concluded the investigators, was real economic devolution to a Scottish Ministry of Industrial Development under an Assembly. In both countries a gulf appeared between the experience of government intervention and the expectations claimed for it. That in itself was to increase disenchantment with Westminster governments.

The fact that Scotland and Wales had higher unemployment rates than England (though the difference between them narrowed in the 1970s) was used by the critics of government policy as a symbol of that failure. But the support for these critics, especially the Nationalists, came not from the unemployed but from the newly enriched, and more, we think, from those who had had their hopes raised. The discovery of oil in large quantities off the coast of Scotland in the late 1960s, and the publicity which was given to this discovery in the 1970s, fitted this mood perfectly. Once the oil had been discovered and valued it was easy for the SNP to ask 'Rich Scots or Poor British' and for its compaigning slogan 'It's Scotland's Oil' to increase the SNP's vote and its membership. The Welsh Nationalists were not so lucky. They came a poor fourth in the October 1974 election while in Scotland the SNP came second (in votes). But then Wales, as we have seen, did not enjoy the same social changes as Scotland during the 1960s. Wales also lacked a large source of oil or gas. In the more depressed atmosphere of Wales in the mid-1970s the Labour Party still performed well, for its old role as the protector of the unemployed was more necessary in Wales than it was in Scotland.

REFERENCES

1. EVANS, G. in *Welsh Nation*, August 1978, p. 8.
2. THOMAS, BRYNLEY (ed.) *The Welsh Economy* (Cardiff: University of Wales, 1962).
3. *Report of the Committee of Inquiry into the Scottish Economy*, Scottish Council (Development and Industry) 1961, pp. 20, 21.
4. *Ministry of Labour/Department of Employment Gazette*, 1950, 1960, 1970 and 1976.

Chapter four

POLITICAL CHANGE IN SCOTLAND AND WALES

The modernisation of Scotland and Wales has had political consequences. The voting patterns of Scots and Welshmen have changed considerably since the 1966 general election. The evidence suggests that it was those voters who were prised loose from their old affiliations by the changes in Scottish and Welsh society who responded to the promises of the Nationalist parties. In order to see the impact of the social changes on voting behaviour we need to look, first of all, at the electoral history of Scotland and Wales.

The electoral history of the two countries since the beginning of the Second World War can be divided into two periods. There was the period up to 1966 in which the electors of the two countries voted, much as the electors of England voted, for one of the two governing parties. By the end of this first period the Labour Party dominated in Wales – it won 32 of the Principality's 36 parliamentary seats; it also won 46 of Scotland's 71 seats. This was Labour's peak in the two countries. But after the 1966 General Election came a period of rapid shifting in which the voters of the two countries fell away from their previous pattern.

Certainly there were some breaks in the general pattern before this, but these were either flukes – such as high Nationalist voting in parliamentary by-elections during the war-time electoral truce between the major parties – or part of the general British trend and hence not particular to Scotland and Wales. The SNP, for example, captured 41 per cent of the vote in a by-election at Kirkcaldy in 1944 and 51 per cent of the vote (and the seat) in Motherwell in 1945. Similarly, the Plaid performed impressively in by-elections during the war-time truce. It won 25 per cent in Carnarvon and 16 per cent in Neath in 1945. Plaid also had some successes after the war – it won 30 per cent at Ogmore and 20 per cent in Aberdare (both in 1946), but these successes were not followed up in the subsequent general election, and they were, therefore, ignored.

Indeed, in the period up to 1966 the threat to the two-party system in Scotland and Wales came from the Liberal Party. Or rather, the Liberal Party benefited from the drift away from the two parties which began to make itself felt in the 1950s in all the British countries. It performed well in by-elections in England, Scotland and Wales. The SNP did not contest by-elections in the 1950s; Plaid did but it was easily bettered by the Liberals.

The first faint glimmerings of change occurred during the 1959-64 Parliament. The first by-election in that period in which the SNP performed well was at Glasgow Bridgeton in November 1961, when (without Liberal opposition) the party won 18.7 per cent of the vote. In the next year the SNP bettered the Liberals by winning 23.3 per cent in a by-election in West Lothian. But even this did not fundamentally change the position. The Liberals easily bettered the Nationalists in a by-election at Glasgow Woodside in November 1962. The main trend in this period was for the Liberals to perform well throughout the UK. On the whole the Nationalist parties were less successful. This picture was confirmed during the short 1964-66 Parliament. The Liberals won an astonishing 49.2 per cent of the vote at a by-election in Roxburgh, Selkirk and Peebles which the SNP did not even contest. And when the Liberals did not contest Abertillery in 1965 Plaid won only 6.7 per cent of the vote.

The major achievement of the SNP and Plaid during this period was simply to survive. The climate was not propitious. In 1959, when Plaid claimed 250 branches, only six were active. Membership (though membership figures of *all* political parties are suspect) fell from a claimed peak of 7,750 in 1957 to 2,543 in 1962. The SNP had even more trouble. In 1962 it had but two active branches with a membership of twenty or more. At that time it also claimed about 2,000 members. And yet for the SNP the worst was past by 1962. Its impressive poll at West Lothian led to a useful increase in members – the more useful for the fact that the new members were predominantly young. In 1962 too, the SNP appointed a full-time organiser and established constituency organisations (alongside its branches), which made the fighting of parliamentary elections easier. These organisational changes prepared the way for the SNP's electoral success. No party can win seats where it does not put up candidates. Few parties put up candidates where they lack a local organisation. The increased organisation of the SNP (and to a lesser extent of the Plaid) made it possible for the National parties to take advantage of the change in electoral climate which occurred soon after the 1966 general election.

In the first by-election after that general election, at Carmarthen in July, Plaid won the seat from Labour with 39 per cent of the vote. The Liberals were second with 20 per cent. In Glasgow Pollock, at the first Scottish by-election of that parliament, in March 1967, the SNP won a handsome 28.2 per cent of the vote. The Liberals, who became the fourth party in Scotland, won 1.9 per cent. But the SNP's important breakthrough came in November 1967 when the party captured the formerly safe Labour seat of Hamilton. The SNP candidate, Mrs Winifred Ewing, took 46 per cent of the vote. The Liberals had not entered the contest. In both countries success in parliamentary by-elections was followed by advances in local government elections. Plaid's record was little short of remarkable; it succeeded in electing 51 councillors in 1969 and 48 in 1970. The SNP did equally well: in May 1968 it polled 34 per cent of the vote in the municipal elections and won 100 seats. This was a larger gain than had ever been recorded by any party. The SNP also fared well, if not so outstandingly, in 1969 but then began to fall back.

For all that the SNP had made some preparations, the successes of 1968 and 1969 were too much for its machine. Fighting local government elections all over the country was a much more demanding job than concentrating all a party's strength on the occasional by-election. The new task was beyond both National parties. Also, despite the Nationalists' success in finding candidates, many were ill-prepared for what faced them. Most, after all, had no thought that they might win when they accepted their party's nomination. Of these some resigned almost immediately – thus forcing by-elections – which did the party little good. As the SNP's success at local elections was the greater, its subsequent fall was the harder. In the 1970 general election the two National parties were able to contest more seats than ever before: Plaid contested all 35 Welsh seats where it had fought only 20 in 1966, and the SNP contested 65 Scottish seats where it had had 23 candidates in 1966. But whereas the Plaid put up its votes per candidate from 3,053 in 1966 to 4,862 in 1970, the SNP won fewer votes per candidate in 1970 than it had in 1966: the figure dropped from 5,585 to 4,535. For both parties the 1970 results were less than the earlier success had promised, but both had grown considerably in members, branches, and experience and both were now being watched warily by the British parties.

The electoral fortunes of the National parties in Scotland and Wales – both their rise immediately after the 1966 election and their disappointment at the 1970 election – were part of a British trend. Voters turned away from the major parties all over Britain after March 1966 but returned in time for June 1970. In some ways the turning away was more noticeable in England than in Scotland and Wales. With the exception of the Carmarthen by-election (July 1967), the turnout in Scotland and Wales at by-elections in this Parliament did not drop by more than 3 per cent (and in three by-elections it was actually higher than at the preceding general election). In England, by way of contrast, turnout at by-elections dropped considerably. In 1967 it was down by an average of 12 per cent, in 1968 by 15 per cent, and in 1969 by 18 per cent and in 1970 by 10 per cent. The smaller drop in the peripheral countries suggests that voters there had found something they positively wanted to vote for in a way which English voters had not. It also suggests that once the Nationalist surge was recognised in Carmarthen, voting in Scotland and Wales became more interesting, for there were few seats safe against the Nationalist tide.

But, just as it would be wrong to isolate the rapid changes occurring in Scotland and Wales from those taking place in England, neither must we assume that the same thing was happening in both Scotland and Wales. The Scottish Nationalists performed much better in the late 1960s than the Welsh Nationalists. This was quite a change in itself from the previous pattern in which the Welsh showed the Scots the way. But when the economic promises of British governments exceeded their performances so that voters all over Britain moved away from the two parties, and when British governments tried to propitiate opinion in Scotland and Wales by conceding measures of local economic management and planning to the two countries, it was the SNP which was better poised to benefit from the opportunity. The SNP put itself forward, as we have seen, more unequivocally as an economic party. It emphasised the way it would use the powers of the state to make Scotland wealthier. Plaid faced the more complicated task of explaining that it wanted to get away from big government and work from the basis of a not entirely clear community power.

The SNP promised Scots what Labour, under Harold Wilson, promised Britons, that it would use the machinery of government to make the nation (the nation concerned varied of course) more prosperous. Moreover the SNP was guided, if not dominated, by men of business and commercial experience. Anyone could see that they could run an establishment. Bardic poets may lack this quality. The SNP had, by the mid-1960s, the advantage of having thought about its economic plans for nearly two decades. Plaid on the other hand was still dominated by *literati* and hesitant in making economic promises. It was thus less attractive to those whose aspirations had been raised and then dashed by British governments. The SNP was in a position to link the economic grievances of many Scots to a ready-made solution,

Scottish independence. The Scottish economy, the argument ran, would be better run by Scots themselves. It was hard in the late 1960s (and later) to think that it might be worse managed than it was by Westminster.

By the middle 1960s the SNP had experience and practice at exploiting economic dissatisfaction. Their first major showing at a by-election was in West Lothian in 1962. Their campaign was fought on the issue of the 'economic and social murder' of the shale oil and coal industries in Scotland. The SNP candidate, Mr William Wolfe, told electors

Less than one hundred years ago Scotland was the wealthiest nation in the world. The decline of the Scottish economy dates back to the 1914–18 war . . . the real beginning of heavy taxation, vast government spending and government control of the economy. We in Scotland are only ten per cent of that economy, so we are relatively unimportant. Your chance of a job in Scotland compared with your chance in England: 6 to 1 against. Your chance of unemployment in Scotland compared with your chance in England: 5 to 2 on.[1]

A Social and Economic Enquiry of Scotland was set up in 1962 principally by Scottish Nationalists. In 1963 the SNP launched their manifesto on the mining industry: 'Room for improvement – the SNP's answer for coal'. In the next two years Nationalists exploited redundancies and the rundown rail, air transport, and the other heavy industries of Scotland. When the SNP published its document *The SNP and You* it said:

We turn envious eyes upon the spacious cities of little lands which ought, by all the arguments of the Westminster politicians, to be poor and wretched. We think of Stockholm and Copenhagen, Oslo and Amsterdam, and then compare Glasgow and Edinburgh and other places with their wretched slums and we look south to England where wages are so much higher and wealth so much more plentiful at our expense, for there is no doubt that we subsidise England under unionist rule – Tory, or Liberal or Labour – and that we help to keep London and Birmingham rich and help to keep unemployment there down to one-quarter of the Scottish rates.[2]

The Nationalist case in Scotland was built upon one major plank, London mismanagement. Discrimination was being practised against Scotland by Westminster Governments. Scotland, the SNP argued, required more resources to attract more industries to create more jobs in a more attractive environment. If the Labour Government's socialism after 1964 was little more than quantitative, promising better economic opportunities and more social welfare, the gist of Nationalist economics was merely to add a few noughts to any demands. The case against economic discrimination was put forward in the Nationalist research publication *Scotland – Facts and Comparisons*, first published in 1969, and the argument for more resources was the essence of the member for Hamilton's contribution to the House of Commons after 1967 – the body of which was published in her 'Black Book' on Whitehall. In her introduction Mrs Ewing stated:

We in the Scottish National Party are also building up a cross-reference of economic detail which demonstrates without doubt that Scotland compares unfavourably with the other small countries in Europe. In other words with our own government we could soon be much more prosperous. We could change the whole quality of life if we were in full control of our country. There is no doubt – despite the fact that governments always refuse to release certain relevant facts – that there is an outflow of many millions each year for which Scotland gets no return[3]

There was sufficient official evidence to disprove the Nationalist claims. After a Scottish Budget was published by the Treasury in 1968, Labour politicians could emphasise that Scotland was receiving more than her per capita share of United Kingdom resources. But by the late 1960s, the Nationalists were propagating their own alternative economic policy statements for a Scottish economy. The sudden discovery of oil lent credibility to these arguments. Oil gave the SNP a psychological boost. From then onwards they shifted from denouncing Westminster policies to stressing the opportunities and self-confidence which independence would generate. By 1975 the Nationalists had developed comprehensive policies for all areas of social and economic life in nineteen major statements approved by their Annual Conferences.

The Welsh National Party was not so well prepared with economic arguments. In the late 1950s it had begun to accommodate itself to the need to appeal for the votes of non-Welsh-speaking Welshmen, but mainly by changing its language policy: at that time it modified its language policy to support for bi-lingualism – rather than for Welsh as the only language. At the 1959 general election, the economic case for self-government took third place to the party's main aim to re-awaken the 'Welshness of the Welsh people.' Economically, the party favoured industrial and agricultural cooperatives as the basic units of economic management. Policy pronouncements on economic matters were restricted to demanding Welsh devolution for the nationalised industries and state agencies involved in economic development.

After the Carmarthen by-election the party set up a Research

Group to assemble an economic programme for Wales. But it took the stimulus of electoral success in local government elections in the southern areas of economic decline to prompt the party to work seriously at an economic programme: only then did they respond to the grievances of Welsh workers, particularly over pit closures. This new emphasis on the economy was confirmed in the policy statements of the late 1960s when the existence of the Welsh Language Society allowed more stress to be placed on economic and social matters. The resulting proposals – ironically rooted in the growthmanship ethos of the Labour Government – favoured the creation of new growth areas in Wales and a massive programme of capital investment in Welsh industry and the economic infrastructure. This implied a managerial approach to the problems of power and was thus at odds with the party's previous commitment to syndicalism. Enemies of the new position could accuse its proponents of searching for jobs at any price. The proposals were debated with some heat in 1968 and 1969, when a diluted version of the original proposals was accepted. Despite the promptings of recent recruits from the industrial parts of Wales like Dr Phil Williams, the party was still not attuned to the economic discontents of its countrymen. In 1969, for instance, the party showed it had some way to go by endorsing an economic plan which favoured selective employment taxes as a key income earner for a future Welsh government and then opposing Selective Employment Tax in principle – or perhaps it was just becoming as confused on economic issues as any large party.

In October 1974, it is true, Plaid decided to copy the SNP's propaganda techniques by putting the question 'Rich Welsh or Poor British?' to the forefront of their election literature. Shortly afterwards, however, the party reversed this change and re-emphasised its syndicalism. And yet, throughout the 1974–79 Parliament the party's monthly paper *Welsh Nation* did as good a job as any political paper in the country in pointing to the economic benefits which came to Wales as the result of Plaid Cymru MPs' pressures on the Labour Government.

In the February 1974 election the SNP won 7 seats with 22 per cent of the vote in Scotland. This was an impressive performance, which paralleled the Liberals' success in polling 21.3 per cent of the English vote. Plaid did not fare so well. It won 2 seats with 11 per cent of the Welsh vote. The SNP went on to confirm its strength and outperform any of the other 'minor' parties in the October 1974 election. Most of the minor parties dropped votes. The SNP gained. It won 30 per cent of the Scots vote and 11 seats, took more votes than the Conservatives in Scotland and stood menacingly second to Labour in 35 out of her 41 seats. As in February, the SNP outperformed Plaid. The Welsh party lost a small number of votes but gained a seat in the House of Commons.

From that point on it was the Scottish National Party which made the running and which served to frighten the British parties the more. For the time being at least the Welsh party played second fiddle. But the achievement of the SNP in becoming the second party in Scotland was not simply an electoral feat. It was seen as a direct challenge to the continued existence of the United Kingdom, for the SNP's professed goal was Scottish independence. And if the 30 per cent of Scottish voters who supported the Nationalists were really voting for a separate state, it was unlikely that secession could be long avoided. On the other hand, if the Nationalist vote was simply a protest vote, it might be contained.

Thanks to the work of Ivor Crewe and his colleagues at the University of Essex, we are able to put the Nationalist achievement into a British perspective (and we are able partly to compensate for the lack of reliable historical data on the voting patterns of Scottish electors).[4] Crewe's work speaks of the 'dealignment' of British electors from the Conservative and Labour parties. It suggests that between 1964 and 1974 the proportion of the British electorate who identified 'very strongly' with either the Conservative or the Labour parties fell from 40 per cent to 24 per cent. He also discovered that while three-quarters of the population still identified themselves with one or other party to some degree, only half the population voted for the party they identified with. Attachment to the two major parties was particularly weak among those who in 1974 were under thirty. There has also been a weakening of class alignment in politics. Crewe found that only half of British working-class voters supported Labour, while on the other hand half the middle-class voters supported it. Indeed, Britons are increasingly reluctant to consider themselves as members of classes. Finally, the voters tended not to share the ideologies, policies and attitudes of the two major parties. This was particularly true of Labour, whose supporters no longer embraced the central tenets of the socialist ideology and were resentful of the power of the trade unions.

All these qualitative changes in the attitudes and orientation of the electorate were observed in Scotland and Wales. The difference between these countries and England was that nationalism offered a different but ready-made basis of allegiance. Thus, the first conclusion that can be reached about Nationalist voting is critical also to the devolution equation: a very substantial minority of those voting for the

SNP and Plaid Cymru probably do not support the major policy of these parties, the creation of separate states. They are likely to favour devolution of power from Westminster, but even then their vote may not owe very much to this belief. Indeed, it seems that even among those who favour independence support for it is often conditional, dependent on the voter's assessment of the balance of economic advantage. This is particularly true in Scotland, where it appears that a majority of those who support independence do so because of the economic benefits they consider would follow. A 1977 Gallup Poll found that while 50 per cent would support independence if there were material advantages, only 12 per cent would do so as a recognition of Scottish identity. That confirmed the findings of a previous survey which established that only 12 per cent in Scotland and 9 per cent in Wales of those who supported constitutional change would do so if it meant they were worse off economically as a result. Thus only a minority of Nationalist voters would appear to be unconditionally attached to the cause of independence.

A second feature of Nationalist voting is that while Nationalist voters tend to share certain attitudes, there is a great deal that divides them. For many Nationalist voters their electoral choice has been tactical: in Conservative seats, Labour sympathisers have voted Nationalist if the SNP was the only serious alternative to the Conservatives. In the North-East of Scotland, for example, the Conservative vote rose in 1974 in the four seats that they lost to the SNP. What had caused the loss to the Nationalists was the defection of Labour and Liberal voters.

On the face of it Nationalist support at successive elections has appeared evenly spread among social classes and income groupings. On closer analysis, however, two features are noticeable. First, Nationalist support is greatest among the most socially mobile sections of the population. Those who have benefited most by the changes in Scottish and Welsh society are, in effect, voting for more of the same kind of change. They are the more optimistic elements in Scotland and Wales. Secondly, certain other groups in society, noticeably the poorest, have been resistant to the charms of Nationalism. This at least was the pattern in the two 1974 general elections. These people, especially when they were also Catholics, were slower to move away from the comforting safety of their old allegiances. During the October 1974 general election their loyalty to the Labour Party in Scotland was the one sure thing which stood between that party's success and its collapse.

Resistance to voting for the SNP in October 1974 when they polled

30 per cent of the vote, was greatest amongst Catholics (11% SNP), trade union members (26% SNP), low income earners (22%), unskilled or semi-skilled workers (20% SNP), house owners (19% SNP), Episcopalians (19% SNP) and the elderly. Resistance came, in other words, from entrenched Labour and Conservative voters. Evidence for Wales in 1974 was more scanty. Evidence for 1979, however, when the Nationalist vote had fallen, showed a pattern similar to that of Scotland.[5] The National party was less favoured by AB voters as well as by DE voters. It won less than its national share among voters who were more than fifty-five years old and less than its average among non-Welsh-speakers.

Two things are clear about voting patterns in Scotland and Wales. One is that there is no strong connection between belief in devolution and voting. Support for the devolution proposals of the 1974–79 Labour Government came (in Scotland) in roughly equal proportions from Labour and SNP voters: Conservatives were the odd men out in being opposed to devolution. The obverse of this is also important: support for devolution does not explain Nationalist voting. Some devolutionists support the National parties, some support the other parties. Our suggestion is that an additional element is necessary to produce National party voting (though the evidence is so scanty that this must remain just a suggestion), namely, that National party voters came in considerable proportion from those who had benefited from the economic changes which had occurred in Scotland, and to a lesser extent, in Wales, but who felt cheated that it had not gone further. They wanted more and the National parties – especially the SNP – promised it.

With this kind of electoral support we can see why the leaders of the SNP have to be so careful not to become identified with either Labour or the Conservatives. Their voters are people who find the Left/Right split, previously so deep in Scotland, anathema. The evidence of opinion polls also stresses the singular importance which the widespread feeling of Scottish nationality has had for the National Party. It is the attraction of attaching themselves to a party which appeals to them as Scots rather than commitment to any particular constitutional proposals which pulls people to the National Party. Were Scottish national pride not so strong, the SNP could never have come so far.

The second thing which is clear about Scottish and Welsh voting is that it is extremely unstable. Voters moved in large numbers into the Nationalist camps in 1974 and in even larger numbers (we think) in 1977, only to move back out again in 1978 and 1979. Labour was the major beneficiary of the move away from the Nationalists in 1978 (in by-elections) and the Conservatives were the major beneficiary in 1979 (in the referendums and the general election). As the Labour government's devolution proposals made their way through the House of Commons voters in Scotland and Wales returned to that party. Then voters in Wales overwhelmingly defeated devolution in the referendum while Scots were nearly evenly split. After the referendum the Conservative party scored victories in rural Wales, which had eluded it for the entire twentieth century, in May 1979; in Scotland Labour capped its progress winning one seat from the Tories and two from the SNP, while the Conservatives reasserted their position as the second party in Scotland and won back all the seats they had lost to the SNP. Whatever the reasons for the volatility of the vote there is no sign that it has calmed down. There is no more reason to think the SNP's unpopularity of 1979 (actually it won 17% of the vote – a considerable improvement on 1970) will last any longer than its previous popularity. Having broken from its old moorings the electorate is being very choosy about its nightly berths.

REFERENCES

1. WOLFE, W. *Scotland Lives* (Edinburgh: Reprographia Ltd.), p. 24.
2. Scottish National Party. *The SNP and You.*
3. EWING, WINIFRED *Scotland and Whitehall* (Edinburgh: SNP 1968) p. vi.
4. CREWE, I. 'Dealignment in British politics 1964–74', *British Journal of Political Science*, 1977, pp. 129–90.
5. BALSOM, D. *BBC Wales Poll*, Sept. 1978, and Feb. 1979, Abacus Research Associates.

Part two
PRESSURES FOR CHANGE

Chapter five

THE ROYAL COMMISSION ON THE CONSTITUTION

Harold Wilson once remarked, in a different context, that a Royal Commission would 'take minutes and spend years'. It may reasonably be said that the Royal Commission on the Constitution appointed by Home Secretary James Callaghan was appointed to do just that. The Government had barely discussed its remit and was far from committed to changing the constitution, but wanted an excuse to do nothing in the face of Nationalist success in the by-elections in Scotland and Wales. For the period that the Commission sat the Government had an unimpeachable excuse for taking no action and producing no plans. It would not do to prejudice the report of the Commission. On the other hand it could be expected that the Commission would be slow to produce its report. Indeed, as if to underline this point, the Government wasted some months between the announcement of the Commission in the autumn of 1968 and the appointment of its members in April 1969. In the event the Commission took four years: it reported in 1973. In the meantime (in 1972) its Chairman, Lord Crowther, had died and was replaced by Lord Kilbrandon. The Commission's Report is popularly known by the name of its second Chairman.

We should not be misled by Sir Harold's cynicism into thinking that the only purpose of Royal Commissions is to get Governments out of tight political corners. Royal Commissions can generate concern about hitherto unpublicised injustices. They can be used to involve interest groups in the preparation of policies which they might otherwise reject if Governments put them forward 'cold'. They collect information which can sometimes be invaluable to later students of their subject (this last is certainly true of the Kilbrandon Report). Nevertheless, Kilbrandon was a Commission designed in the words of the Secretary of State for Scotland, Mr William Ross (who was no less cynical than his Prime Minister) to 'kill devolution'.

The Commission's terms of reference did not specifically mention either Scotland or Wales, and neither did they mention devolution:

Whereas by Warrant under Our Royal Sign Manual bearing date the fifteenth day of April, 1969, We authorised and appointed you to be a Commission to examine the present functions of the central legislature and government in relation to the several countries, nations and regions of the United Kingdom; to consider, having regard to developments in local government organisation and in the administrative and other relationships between the various parts of the United Kingdom, and to the interests of the prosperity and good government of Our people under the Crown, whether any changes are desirable in those functions or otherwise in present constitutional and economic relationships; to consider, also, whether any changes are desirable in the constitutional and economic relationships between the United Kingdom and the Channel Islands and the Isle of Man[1] ...

Despite this brief, the Commission decided that it should interpret its terms of reference to mean a consideration of a change in the constitutional status of Scotland and Wales. The Government had been too polite to say that it was responding to the political pressure of votes for the SNP and Plaid Cymru, but this was the fact of the matter and the Commission's majority decided to acknowledge it.

The membership of the Commission hinted more accurately than the formal remit what the Commission was to be about. The half of the UK population which lives in the southern part of England (the Midlands, the South-East and East Anglia) was represented by three of the eleven Commissioners who signed the final report. There were two members each from Scotland, Wales, the North of England and one each from Northern Ireland and the South-West of England. The opening paragraphs of the Report make it clear that the majority of the commissioners had taken the political point of their appointment: they had been asked how to deal with the separatist parties.

1. In 1969, when we were appointed, there was obviously some discontent with the working of government. ...

2. People in Scotland, their normal political loyalties shaken, had begun to rally in substantial numbers behind the banner of the Scottish National Party. ...

3. The picture in Wales was very similar. ... People felt frustrated at their own inability to influence the situation (of rapid industrial change). As in Scotland, this frustration found expression in a sharp rise in support for a nationalist party, Plaid Cymru, which pressed the case for self-government.[2]

Much is given away by the description of Scots voters' previous preferences as 'normal'. The task of the Commission was to find a way to bring the voters back to their normal home and away from their current aberration.

From the first the Commission was sceptical in its questions to the representatives of the National parties. The first examination of witnesses occurred in Wales. The Commission sat in Cardiff on 15 and 16 September 1969. Apart from testiness on both sides over the length of the Plaid's presentations (Lord Crowther thought they were too long), and annoyance on both sides about Plaid's insistence on giving some of its evidence in Welsh (Plaid wanted simultaneous translation services and the Commission objected to being given only twenty-four hours notice of this problem) the tenor of the discussion was sceptical rather than hostile. It is easy to read the *Minute of Evidence* now and convince oneself that this was because the demands made by the Welsh Party were so unworldly. This is illustrated in the following interrogation of the Plaid spokesmen by Mr Houghton.

143. .... *I have not noticed that we were welcomed here by a large crowd saying, 'Independence for Wales: Plaid Cymru for Wales'. I do not think that a single person outside noticed our arrival. ... To what extent is your approach to this politically and economically balanced and not resting upon this inner passion I mentioned earlier?*   Our case is fundamentally a moral case. We are a nation, and we say that whatever the economic consequences would be we should be a self-governing nation, but we have to work within an economic context and work responsibly. We have to show people what the economic consequences are likely to be. We have been trying to do that and honestly produce facts and figures which will assure people of the nature of the economic consequences. We in Wales have had terrible economic experiences. I am old enough myself to remember what happened in the years of the depression, and one cannot go to people and expect them merely to accept your moral arguments....

144. ... *Are you telling the Commission that the Welsh people do not feel sufficiently identified as a nation, as a people, with culture and language and history and traditions, to demand independence for its own sake?*   Yes, I think that is true, ...[3]

Two weeks later, on 29 and 30 September, the Commission found the SNP submissions and their spokesmen altogether less easy to handle. The SNP, in its written submission, asserted that Scotland was a nation and that there was no room to doubt this, that the Scottish nation enjoyed a democratic and legal right to withdraw from the Union, and that this right was not open to question, and that the method of asserting this right should be via the ballot box. In other words the SNP asserted that if a majority of Scottish parliamentary seats fell at the subsequent – or any subsequent – general election to

SNP candidates, these candidates would have the right to negotiate Scottish independence with the UK government and the UK government would have a duty to negotiate with them. The Commission were not impressed.

Its Chairman, in particular, subjected the SNP spokesmen to a series of hostile questions – and found his hostility fully reciprocated. This exchange between Lord Crowther and Dr Robert Macintyre gives the flavour of the session. Crowther speaks first.

505. *Of these three criteria are at any rate some of them not a little difficult to ascertain? let us take them in order: ... how do we know them to be true?* We know that it is true by the general acceptance by the people of Scotland ... that Scotland is a nation.

506. *How do we know that there is such acceptance?* There was such an acceptance in connection with the Royal Commission under Lord Balfour [which sat on devolution in 1952].

507. *What form did general acceptance take?* A statement which was made by Lord Balfour that Scotland was a nation and was to be treated as a nation.

508. *And that in your opinion is conclusive?* No, it is evidence.

509. *I am Chairman of this Commission; if I state that Scotland is not a nation, is that equally conclusive?* No, sir, because you are not in a position to make such a statement. You are not a Scotsman.

510. *Distance may lend objectivity* Perhaps we could take you over.[4]

Nor did the Commission like the resemblance between the SNP's evidence and the Unilateral Declaration of Independence (UDI) of the white regime in Rhodesia:

549. *You say that if certain conditions are established that would satisfy you, and you would 'expect' – that is your word – Parliament to repeal the Act of Union. Have the English no say in the matter?* With respect, there is not an Act of Union, although I know that our evidence does speak in those terms. If I may correct that, it should be either 'the Union legislation' ... or more simply, 'the Treaty of Union'.

550. *Would you accept that, since it takes two or more parties to make a union, it also takes two or more parties to dissolve one?* No of course I would not. It has been proved so often that a unilateral declaration of independence is effectively and legally as proper as an agreed, negotiated one.

551. *This is a matter in which nothing succeeds like success.* True, revolution succeeds.

552. *Would it be accepted in England as a reasonable proposition that, if Scotland has spoken, then without further demur or discussion the union legislation should be repealed* Are you suggesting that the English people are not sufficiently

civilised to recognise natural right, which is so acceptable in other parts of the world, and which England herself has accepted in relation to many other countries in the last twenty years?[5]

Although the SNP evidence which formed the basis for this examination was very general in tone and did not lay out the specific grievances the Scots had against the Union, it did mention one specific case: there were no direct commercial flights between Edinburgh and Europe. The Commission had much fun pointing out how trivial this complaint was.

There was little difficulty in the Commission's examination of the STUC or the Scottish Council of the Labour Party. The STUC's evidence was not terribly impressive because the STUC had changed its mind while the Commission was sitting. Originally, it had been opposed to legislative devolution; subsequently it declared in favour. The Scottish Council of the Labour Party expressed itself well satisfied with the status quo. Indeed, much of its testimony took the form of saying that the current Secretary of State for Scotland, Mr Ross, was so determined that he was better for Scotland than any Assembly would ever be. The Welsh Council of the Labour Party, on the other hand, was in favour of a devolved Assembly for Wales, and stuck to its position.

When the Commissioners pointed out to the Scottish Council of the Labour Party that they were out of step with their Welsh brothers, the answer they received was interesting: Scotland was well enough governed because it had the Scottish Office. This points to a division in Scotland between the devolvers and the anti-devolvers. Those who favour the creation of an elected Assembly do not believe that the operations of the Scottish Office were being sufficiently scrutinised by a democratically elected body. Those who are opposed to elective devolution think that control of the Scottish Office by the Westminster government is more satisfactory to Scotland than any division of powers between that government and an elected Assembly could be. A reading of the evidence of the officials from the Scottish and Welsh Offices lends some colour to this argument: the Scottish Office people (particularly the Scottish Development Department witnesses – not so much the Scottish Education Department witnesses) knew their arguments and made light work of the Commissioners' questions. The newer Welsh Office civil servants did not. At one point the Scottish Office spokesman came very close to claiming that his department spoke for Scotland against the Treasury, rather than (which would be constitutionally correct) for the Treasury in Scotland. The spokesman for the Welsh Office had frequently to admit that his recently (1964) established office was just working itself into its new role.

The truth is that the Commission was not a happy one. Three of its members resigned, Selwyn Lloyd on becoming Speaker of the House of Commons and David Basnett and Douglas Houghton without formal explanation in August 1971 and March 1973 respectively. Two other members of the original Commission died during the course of its deliberations. In November 1970 Professor A. T. Peacock was appointed to fill the vacancy caused by the death of Professor D. J. Robertson; Lord Crowther was replaced as Chairman by Lord Kilbrandon in March 1972.

The members of the Royal Commission were united in thinking that something had to be done but they divided on the kind of reforms that were desirable. They split into two main groups, with the minority supporting a scheme for devolution to all the regions. The majority commissioners were also divided amongst themselves on matters of detail. Their Report was messy, with minor objections inserted in unexpected places. This was unfortunate and unusual. Royal Commissions usually go to great lengths to accommodate individual members since it is on fact that members representing diverse interests have reached agreement that the authority of their reports depends. But, in this case, mainly because of the large number of resignations and the death of the Chairman late in the proceedings, the Commission did not present a united front.

The main body of the report proposed a form of devolution for Scotland and Wales. But it did not plunge right into this proposal. It began, instead, with a three-part division of constitutional forms. It argued that separatism, federalism and devolution must be distinguished.

'Separatism' was its pejorative characterisation of the proposals that Scotland and Wales should be independent countries. The term reminded readers that in this event these countries would be separate from England. To describe the aspirations of some Scots and Welshmen to have their own countries as 'separatism' was deliberately unflattering. As Kilbrandon put it:

We are concerned here with the general concept of separatism, not merely with the particular proposals of the Scottish National Party and Plaid Cymru. We use the term to mean the separation of Scotland and Wales from the rest of the United Kingdom and their conversion into fully independent sovereign states with complete control over all their internal and external affairs. In accordance with our terms of reference we assume that as independent states they would remain under the Crown. They would be fully self-governing members of the Commonwealth.[6]

The Commissioners could not accept that this was a good idea. They argued that the National parties based their case for the independence of their countries on the distinctive nationalism of their peoples. The Commissioners did not deny the distinctive nationality of the Scottish and Welsh peoples, but held that this did not lend support to the argument for independence for three reasons. Firstly, because Scots and Welshmen were, in effect, dual-nationals. Most of them were, and according to the Commission, are proud of being both Scots or Welsh and British. Secondly, because the administrative devolution already introduced went a considerable way towards giving the Scots and Welsh a distinctive pattern of government – one which was sensitive to the distinctive needs and traditions of the peoples of these countries. Finally, the Commissioners felt that nothing should be done which would disturb the essential unity of the United Kingdom (as the devolution debate progressed this phrase 'the essential unity of the United Kingdom' was to become a shibboleth amongst anti-devolvers). If that term had a precise meaning, it was never explained.

Kilbrandon was careful to argue that the economic viability of an independent Scotland or Wales was a secondary matter. There was unlikely to be much difference in the standard of living of the people of either country if independence was achieved. Nevertheless, the Kilbrandon Commission did think that both countries would be a little poorer than they were. They accepted Treasury estimates that Scotland and Wales were net beneficiaries of public expenditure, that they received more in grants, pensions, and other forms of public expenditure than they contributed to the Treasury in taxation. This account did not, however, take any serious measure of the value of North Sea oil. Kilbrandon realised that if there were a great deal of oil in the sea–bed off the shores of Scotland and if Scotland were granted control of these assets as part of an independence settlement, that might substantially change the argument. But such calculations, the Commission was firmly convinced, were a secondary matter. The first question, they asserted, was whether or not the Scottish and Welsh people really wanted independence. They didn't.

Much the same reason was found for rejecting federalism. No-one wanted it. As the report said:

There is very little demand for federalism in Scotland and Wales, and practically none at all in England. Few of our witnesses advocated it, and people who know the system well tend to advise against it. Nevertheless, it is an important constitutional model midway between separatism, which we reject, and devolution, which in one form or another we favour.[7]

The Commission had been warned by one of its researchers not to try to define federalism. Such definitions were often meaningless. Nevertheless, the Commission did briefly describe federalism:

In a federal system sovereignty is divided between two levels of government. The federal government is sovereign in some matters and the provincial governments are sovereign in others. Each within its own sphere exercises its power without control from the other and neither is subordinate to the other. It is this feature which distinguishes a federal from a unitary constitution. In the latter all sovereignty rests with the central government; if provincial governments exist, they are subordinate authorities, deriving their power from the central legislature, which may overrule them at any time by the ordinary legislative processes.[8]

It went on to point out that federalism was a nineteenth-century invention and that many federal countries were having difficulty in maintaining the independence of the lower tier of government. The central governments had superior tax-raising powers and this eventually led, in most federal countries, to their dominating the lower tier. It also found an objection to federalism in the fact that a federal constitution was inevitably a written constitution and this was foreign to British experience, that England was so much bigger than either Scotland or Wales that it would dominate the other two, and that any federal constitution would endanger the undivided sovereignty of parliament. This the Commission wanted to avoid. The Commission then turned to consider devolution. Firstly, it defined devolution:

543. The transfers of power with which we shall be concerned in this and subsequent parts of our Report, therefore, are those which would leave overriding control in the hands of Parliament. The extent of the powers transferred and the conditions under which they were to be exercised would be prescribed by statute and might at any time be changed by Parliament or by Ministers answerable to it. In other words we shall be concerned with devolution, which is the delegation of central government powers without the relinquishment of sovereignty.[9]

The Commission were aware that several different kinds of devolution were possible: legislative devolution, in which an Assembly would have the right to make law in specified areas; executive devolution, in which an Assembly would have the right to execute certain of the laws passed by Parliament: and advisory devolution, in which an Assembly would have the right to advise others on the formulation of policy.

Six of the members of the Commission recommended a form of devolution for Scotland and Wales which would give their Assemblies powers in all three spheres. Each Assembly would have about 100 members, who would be directly elected. The Assembly would choose its own executive. It would have power over local government, town and country planning, new towns, housing, building control, water supply and sewerage, ancient monuments and historic buildings; over roads, road passenger transport and harbours; over education (excluding universities), over youth and community services, sport and recreation, arts and culture; over social services and health; over some parts of agriculture, forestry, Crown estates and tourism. The Scottish Assembly was, in addition, to have control of the police, fire service, criminal policy and administration and prisons; the administration of justice and legal matters, including law reform; Highlands and Islands development and sea transport. The list of powers devolved was similar to the powers exercised at the time for Scotland and Wales by the Scottish and Welsh Offices. The special additions for Scotland were a reflection of Scotland's separate legal system and the existing control over it by the Scottish Office.

The Commission recommended that the new Assemblies enjoy the greatest financial scope consistent with the political and economic unity of the United Kingdom. There would be an Exchequer Board (i.e. a body independent of both Westminster and the devolved Assemblies) which would decide after receiving estimates from both Westminster and the Assemblies how much money each Assembly needed to maintain the same standards in the devolved services as were maintained in those services in the rest of the UK. The Assemblies were to be able to transfer money from one account to another in accord with their own policies.

The majority of the Kilbrandon Commission considered that the establishment of such Assemblies would go a long way to alleviating the feelings of the Scottish and Welsh people of being remote from government. The Assemblies would have control over many of the areas of government responsibility which affected ordinary citizens. But, the majority thought, once such Assemblies were established there would be no case for the retention by the Scottish and Welsh people of their disproportionately large number of MPs, nor for the retention of the Secretaries of State for Scotland and Wales in the Cabinet. Accordingly the number of MPs for Scotland should be reduced from 71 to 57 and for Wales from 36 to 31. The two offices of Secretary of State would disappear.

The majority of the Commission based their report, to surprising extent, on a single argument: Scotland and Wales should have devolved Assemblies because the Scottish and Welsh people wanted them. Their warrant for saying this came from a series of public opinion surveys which they had commissioned. The opinion polls were carried out in the winter of 1969–70. In fact, the results of the polls hardly bore out the majority report at all. For instance, one survey revealed that 62 per cent of British people were satisfied with the way the government was run and more people were dissatisfied with local than central government. Furthermore, only 3 per cent of those polled spontaneously suggested that they would like people in their region to have more say in the way the region was run when asked how the government of their region could be improved (Scotland and Wales counting here as regions): 21 per cent wanted better roads, 20 per cent wanted better leisure facilities, and 20 per cent wanted more economic development.

The Commission's use of its survey data was odd in two ways. In the first place their evidence had been asked for and collected nearly four years before the report was published. It is one thing to argue that opinion polls over a long period have shown, say, that the Scottish and Welsh people favour a measure of devolution, but quite another to argue from one set of polls that there is public support for this important constitutional change. The use of the survey evidence was also odd in the way it ignored complaints from England, particularly from the North. The truth is that the Commission's own polls showed that dissatisfaction with Westminster government increased with the distance from Westminster. It was therefore stronger in Northern England than in Wales. That being so, there could be no argument from the survey evidence for a scheme of devolution to Wales without a similar proposal for the North of England. But, of course, the Commission was not really concerned with its own survey evidence. It was reacting to the threat to the Conservative and Labour parties – not to mention to the United Kingdom – posed by the rise of the Scottish and Welsh National parties. The reason why the majority of the Commission did not propose devolution to the North of England was that there was not effective political demand for it. The survey evidence was just a smoke-screen.

This was seen by the authors of the Memorandum of Dissent, Lord Crowther-Hunt (no relation of the first Chairman), an Oxford politics don, and Professor A. T. Peacock, an economist from York. The authors of the Memorandum went back to the Commission's brief and interpreted it more literally than the authors of the majority report. Like the authors of the majority report, the authors of the

Memorandum proposed a system of devolution which would involve legislative, executive and advisory powers. The main difference, however, was that the social scientists thought it important for the unity of the UK as well as for simple justice to its citizens that whatever rights were extended to the citizens of Scotland and Wales were also extended to all other UK citizens. They therefore proposed the establishment of seven regional assemblies, one each for Scotland and Wales and one for each of five English regions. These assemblies would have roughly the powers suggested for the Scottish and Welsh authorities by the rest of the Commission. They would also have the right to raise tax by a sales tax or by a surcharge on income tax. The Memorandum, in keeping with its remit, did not confine itself to devolution and suggested other improvements in the constitution such as the creation of more subject committees in the House of Commons.

There is a curious symmetry about the majority and minority reports. The majority report understood the political problem – the rise of the National parties in Scotland and Wales – to which it was asked to propose a solution. But it hardly went further than this. The proposals which it made were backed by only the thinnest of theoretical or administrative arguments. Could devolution to two parts of the United Kingdom ever lead to a re-establishment of stability? The minority report saw the need for making proposals which had a kind of constitutional logic behind them and the minority authors addressed themselves more literally to the remit of the whole Commission. But the minority report was utterly devoid of political sense. Why should the English be given a tier of government which nobody wanted and to which only the most lukewarm local sentiments attached? Each part of the Report was strong where the other was weak.

The reports were published together in October 1973. Despite their weaknesses they did – or rather the majority report did – provide a blueprint for future reform. The Commissioners gave heavyweight sanction to a change in the constitution which was being pressed by many Nationalists. They also changed the terms of discussion about the British constitution. Kilbrandon put 'devolution' and 'federalism' on to the political agenda, not just in Scotland and Wales but in the whole country. In the first few months after the report was published this was not clear, but it soon became so. The Royal Commission had taken minutes and spent years, but it had kept the debate alive through lean times and did not kill devolution.

REFERENCES

1. Kilbrandon, *Report*, p. iii and iv.
2. *Ibid.*, p. 3.
3. *Ibid.*, Minutes of Evidence, Vol. I (Wales), paras 143, 144, p. 63.
4. *Ibid.*, Minutes of Evidence, Vol. II (Scotland), p. 73.
5. *Ibid.*, Minutes of Evidence, Vol. II (Scotland), p. 76.
6. *Ibid.*, Report, para. 425, p. 133.
7. *Ibid.*, Report, para. 498, p. 152.
8. *Ibid.*, Report, para, 502, p. 152.
9. *Ibid.*, Report, para. 543, p. 165.

Chapter six

OPINION IN THE COUNTRY

The Kilbrandon Commission's arguments for creating devolved legislatures in Scotland and Wales were based to a remarkable degree on the supposed desire of the Scottish and Welsh people for changes.[1] When the House of Commons came to debate the 1974–79 Labour Government's proposals to create such legislatures the arguments of the pro-devolution speakers again rested to a remarkable degree on the same supposed public demand for devolution. The Kilbrandon Commission has been criticised for the way it used its survey evidence, but, that criticism aside, a number of factors do emerge. Opinion in Wales, for one thing, is volatile – it is more volatile than opinion in Scotland. Surveys conducted in 1967 and 1968 in Wales for the *Western Mail* by Opinion Research Centre showed 60 per cent of those polled in favour of a Welsh Parliament for Welsh affairs. On the other hand, a 1977 poll for Harlech Television and the *Western Mail* by Research and Marketing Ltd revealed fewer than 30 per cent in favour of the Government's proposals. A year later, early in 1978, a poll by Abacus for BBC Wales showed 40.8 per cent in favour of devolution. In direct contrast, opinion in Scotland has been remarkably steady. 60 per cent of Scots regularly favoured some form of devolution in polls conducted between 1967 and 1978. The rest of the population was evenly divided between those who favoured the status quo and those who wanted independence. If public opinion were the sole criterion of whether Scotland and Wales should have devolved parliaments, then on the basis of the polls it could have been argued that Scotland should, but that Welsh opinion was not sufficiently settled for a judgement to be made.

Another fact about public opinion, as measured in polls, emerges from the Kilbrandon report and subsequent research: opinion within England varies considerably from region to region. In 1970, for example, a study by David Butler and Donald Stokes tended to confirm Kilbrandon's general conclusion while throwing a new light on it. Butler and Stokes's polls asked their respondents: 'Some people think that government is too much centralised in London. Others are quite content with things as they are. What do you think?' Table 3 shows the answers they received.[2]

Table 1

Answer	London and SE	Mid- lands	South- West	Wales	North	Scotland
Content (%)	72	65	57	55	52	26
Too centralised (%)	21	29	37	38	45	65
Don't know (%)	7	6	6	7	5	9

This confirmation leads to a number of speculations. If it is true that opinion in England varies so markedly from region to region and if devolution is so strongly favoured in the North and North-West of England, should not something be done there too? And, secondly, since nothing is being done, the reason must surely be the lack of a separatist political movement in those areas.

There is, however, another dimension to public opinion. In addition to what people want, there is the question of how much they want it. We have seen from the Kilbrandon evidence that there is reason to doubt whether people even in the country most favourable to devolution – Scotland – care very much about it. Only 3 per cent spontaneously mentioned it to the Kilbrandon survey teams. Similar, though higher, figures have been consistently returned by surveys which ask Scots their priorities for government action. In such surveys 'devolution' or its equivalent normally is mentioned as the eighth or tenth most popular choice with 6–10 per cent of the population mentioning it spontaneously. The low intensity of support for devolution is worth bearing in mind because it makes the response of the Labour and Conservative parties more explicable. They are responding, not so much to public opinion, as to the threat posed to them by the Nationalist parties. They are trying to show the people of Scotland and Wales that they are not less strongly Scottish and Welsh than the Nationalist parties of these countries.

Since the advocates of devolution emphasised the popular support for their proposed change, when its opponents in the House of Commons demanded a referendum to settle the issue, it was difficult to deny them. The anti-devolutionists' move had two facets. On the one hand, they could argue that the referendum in 1975 on British membership of the EEC had created a precedent that important constitutional changes required such popular assent. In addition they saw that, particularly in Wales, support for the Government's proposals was terribly thin. The referenda bore out the antis' view. Wales rejected the Government's proposals by an overwhelming 4 to 1, and even the Scots, previously so solid in their support, only narrowly voted in favour, by 51.8 per cent to 48.5 per cent. We shall discuss the reasons for this later. For the present it is enough to observe that more people began to think about the practical implications of devolution – the cost, the extra civil servants, the possible conflicts between the Assemblies and Parliament – the less they seemed to like it. And such practicalities only came to life when the Bills were there to be discussed and voted on.

The press played an important role in the devolution debate. They may or may not have made – or prevented the making of – converts to the Nationalist parties or to devolution, but certainly they wrote the political agenda. One reason why the response of the political parties to the diffuse pressure for devolution was so strong was that a number of 'serious' newspapers and broadcasting organisations took the issue seriously. Scotland has its own morning newspapers. 84 per cent of newspapers bought in Scotland are printed there. Indeed, each Scottish city has its own morning newspaper. The morning paper of Edinburgh is the *Scotsman*. Glasgow has its *Glasgow Herald*. Both of these papers circulate throughout the central belt of Scotland, but neither has much circulation in the main city of the other. Since the *Glasgow Herald* went down-market after the editorial staff of the *Scottish Daily Express* moved to Manchester, the *Herald* has ceased to carry much political news. It has, however, a circulation of 108,000 and has been consistently cool towards devolution.

The *Scotsman* has a circulation of 89,000 and is largely read in Edinburgh and by the middle classes. The English and Welsh might think of it as something between the *Times* and the *Guardian* for it aspires to the quasi-official position the *Times* once held and to the lively trendiness characteristic of the *Guardian*. It is Scotland's most politically serious newspaper and has strongly supported devolution for many years, while not favouring independence. The *Scotsman* increased its political staff in anticipation of the creation of the Assembly and is proud of being the newspaper of devolution.

The popular press in Scotland does not devote much space to political matters. Nonetheless, it is mostly pro-devolution. The two most popular Scottish papers are the *Daily Record* (circulation 660,808) and the *Scottish Daily Express* (circulation 345,500). During most of the devolution struggle both were sympathetic to devolution as tantamount to being 'for' Scotland and both, at one time, showed some sympathy for the SNP. After Mrs Winnie Ewing's victory in the by-election at Hamilton in 1967, both papers carried regular columns by her. During the debates between 1974 and 1978 about the Government's proposals both took the general line that the proposals were 'not enough'. They urged some control over North Sea oil and some powers of taxation. Indeed, the *Daily Record*, which usually supports the Labour Party in general elections, took such a strong pro-devolution stance in 1976 and 1977 that many expected it to back the Nationalists at the next election. But more recently both papers have moved away from both the Nationalists and from devolution. The *Record* denounced the SNP in the winter of 1978 and the *Express* came out against devolution during the devolution campaign in January 1979.

The radio and television networks in Scotland operate under the legal requirement to be objective and unbiased. This requirement has been fulfilled. But the most exciting Scottish political news in the years since the 1966 General Election has been the rise of the SNP and the related move to devolution. The radio and television networks have fully reported these developments and their Scottish news and current affairs departments have grown as the interest in this Scottish story has increased. The broadcasters are not so much for devolution in a partisan sense as excited by it. In its turn their interest has served the cause of devolution and of the Nationalist party well, because it has helped to keep the Scottish question on the boil. Some anti-devolutionists believe that the BBC is more pro-devolution than the independent stations. More Scots watch independent television than BBC, but the independent output is split into three areas: STV (the central belt); Border (the south) and Grampian (the north).

The *Western Mail* claims to be the 'National newspaper of Wales' and has consistently backed the move to establish the Welsh office and to create an elected Assembly for Wales. Like the *Scotsman*, it has forced the debate upon its readers, but in social terms it is very unlike the *Scotsman*. Nearly half of its 100,000 readers are in rural West Wales, the rest being spread through the country, though it has few readers in North Wales. Its main competitor in its area of circulation is the *Daily Mirror* (when the *Mirror* goes on strike the *Mail* gains circulation). One of its most popular features is its rugby coverage.

Northern Wales is served by the *Liverpool Daily Post*'s Wales edition. This paper has a circulation of about 40,000 in Wales. As it happens, the *Daily Post* circulates in the part of Wales where the Plaid have most of their parliamentary seats, but the paper has not taken a consistent line on devolution. Most of the Welsh read English newspapers.

The Welsh broadcasters operate under the same constitutional constraints as do the Scots. However, the Welsh language movement has been successful in its insistence that the BBC broadcast in both languages in Wales. This success has made it inevitable that most senior broadcasters (though not, as it happens, the BBC political correspondent for Wales) are bilingual. Most bilingual Welshmen are strong nationalists. This is not to say that they are biased, or to suggest that they abuse their positions. But there can be no doubt that they honestly believe the language question and the national question to be of high importance, and this belief is reflected in their work. It is worth noting that the Chairman of the Welsh board of HTV is Mr Alun Talfan Davies, QC, who was a Kilbrandon Commissioner.

The pressure which the press can bring to bear on politicians derives from its apparent ability to affect the terms of public political debate. One powerful school of political commentary now argues that this is no longer the most effective or important way of putting pressure on government. This group of commentators holds that interest groups such as the CBI, the TUC, and individual unions, the National Farmers' Union, the British Medical Association, with Shelter and other voluntary bodies, carry much more weight. Government appears to depend on the good will of such groups because they control crucial parts of the economy or because they possess technical knowledge which the governments need – or because they combine these things with the ability to gain favourable publicity for their cause.

Partly as a result, government has fallen into the habit of discharging some of its executive responsibilities by handing them over to appointed agencies dominated by pressure groups. The Scottish Development Agency, the General Teaching Council, the Historic Buildings Council, the White Fish Advisory Council are such appointed bodies. To its proponents – most notably to Professor John P. Mackintosh in his seminal work *The Devolution of Power* – legislative devolution is partly an attempt to counteract this increasing manipulation of politicians by pressure groups. If the devolutionists are right, it is certainly interesting to look at the reaction of these pressure groups to the devolution proposals.

Perhaps the first thing that needs to be said is that until the Labour Government of October 1974 made it clear in November 1975 that it was going to try to legislate on devolution, the largest pressure groups took the whole thing in a relaxed way. When the Kilbrandon Commission called for evidence, the mighty TUC could only move itself to present a two-page memorandum. More or less politely it told the Commissioners it had more important things to think about than devolution:

The General Council are bound to point out that trade unions have not, at least in modern times, shown great interest in the issues which are being investigated by the Commission: it may be significant that no affiliated union has felt it necessary to initiate a debate on this subject at any Annual Conference in recent years.[3]

And then, somewhat prissily, it laid down the conditions under which it would begin to think about devolution:

Before supporting any move toward devolution the TUC would wish to be satisfied that it would lead to a sustained improvement in working conditions and living standards in the whole of the United Kingdom, that greater control over the social and industrial environment would result from devolution, and that there was a genuine desire among the people for a move towards devolution. The General Council believe that they would be in a better position to evaluate these questions in the light of the Commission's report than on the basis of the information now available.[4]

The CBI took the operation more seriously. It established a working party and also collected evidence separately from Scotland, Wales and Northern Ireland. In general, the CBI was opposed to legislative devolution but thought industry in Scotland, Wales and Northern Ireland had benefited from such administrative devolution as existed and wanted some of the benefits of this system to be available to England as well. A note of disdain, not unlike that of the TUC, did however creep into the Scottish CBI's evidence. It said:

As the Commission will be aware, a proposal is currently being debated for the revival of some form of Scottish Assembly or Parliament. The CBI Council in Scotland has not succeeded in identifying any advantages for industry which such an Assembly would hold out but, on the other hand, we cannot see that any disadvantages would be involved. It is felt however that it would add unnecessarily to the complexities and cost of Government. In our view the trend should be in the direction of reducing the complexity and clarifying the processes of Government.[5]

In comparison with the large number of pressure groups the Commission received few submissions. Private individuals aside, the only groups other than the TUC and the CBI which chose to submit written evidence on a British basis were the Committee of University Vice-Chancellors (opposed to any change), the Electoral Reform

Society and two groups interested in taxation. A number of regional and local English groups submitted evidence, three Cornish Associations, the four Local Government Associations, the Regional Economic Planning Councils, the Northern Arts Association, the Northern Regional Council of the Labour Party, two parts of the Standing Conferences of Local Planning Authorities: all these submitted evidence, as did the Liberal Party. No part of the Conservative Party gave written or oral evidence to the Commission.

Apart from Government departments, political parties and private individuals only six Scottish groups troubled to submit written evidence to Kilbrandon: the Faculty of Advocates (advocates are in Scotland what barristers are in England and Wales), the Law Society of Scotland, the Scottish Law Commission, the Saltire Society, the Scottish Economic Planning Council and the Scottish Plebiscite Society. In addition, the Church and Nation Committee of the Church of Scotland gave written evidence. The Faculty of Advocates stressed the need to remove certain anomalies. It was concerned about 'the inaccessibility of the legislature in Westminster to the people of Scotland, and its remoteness from the formative organs of Scottish public opinion, including the Scottish press and Scottish broadcasting'. The Law Society of Scotland (the solicitors) feared assimilation into the English legal system and recommended a number of minor changes short of 'legislative devolution'. The Scottish Law Commission was of the same mind as the Law Society. The Saltire Society eschewed specific proposals but wanted the Commission 'to find a pattern for the future which will place our cultural life and its instruments – notably education, television and radio as well as the means of publication – much more firmly in Scottish hands'. The Scottish Economic Planning Council was well pleased with the *status quo*. The Scottish Plebiscite Society wanted a plebiscite on any proposals. The Church and Nation Committee gave the only really strong support of legislative devolution. Most groups failed to make any response at all.

One important pressure group, the Scottish Council (Development and Industry) did not submit written evidence because it had submitted a memorandum on the subject of devolution to the House of Commons Select Committee on Scottish Affairs in December 1969. It did, however, send senior spokesmen to testify to the Commission when it met in Edinburgh. The Scottish Council is a microcosm of government in Scotland. The Council was formed in 1946 to help Scottish industry recover from the war and is financed by the Convention of Scottish Local Authorities, companies, banks, chambers of commerce, and trade unions, while its individual projects receive money and other support from the Scottish Office. It performs many services for industry in Scotland, notably through its Scottish Export Committee. This Committee does for Scotland what the Department of Trade's British National Export Council is supposed to do for the whole of Britain. Since BNEC works on behalf of Scotland as well as England, the Scottish Office is not allowed to promote exports to avoid upsetting the balance of export drives within the UK. So, in effect, it has encouraged the growth of a 'private' body which cannot be barred in law from doing what the Scottish Office would not be allowed by the Treasury to do. This is government working with a private self-appointed agency out of sight of the democratically elected legislature. It is just the sort of thing which devolution is meant to stop. The Scottish Council (Development and Industry) proposed to Kilbrandon that the role of its Scottish Export Council be performed by the Board of Trade in Edinburgh. In other words that the function it was performing for central government be performed by central government on a decentralised basis. This proposal was taken to mean more devolution of an administrative kind by the commissioners. Whether it was that or not, the Scottish Council's advice on this matter was the only pro-devolution advice which the Commission received from a group based in industry.

The Welsh pressure groups were more forthcoming than the Scots. Written evidence was received from twelve groups. Anglesey Council wanted a 'National Welsh authority for water supply and distribution'. The Association of Welsh Local Authorities wanted an elected executive and advisory authority. It hoped that such a body might later acquire legislative powers. 'Self-government for Wales' was the guiding principle of the Baptist Union of Wales and the Presbyterian Church agreed. On the other hand, the Welsh Council of the British Medical Association was concerned to preserve professional independence – 'any limitation of the present format would be unwelcome, unwise and detrimental to standards'. These views were seconded by the Welsh Committee for Hospital Medical Services. A specifically pro-devolution group, the Cathays Group, wanted a form of devolution like that which the Commission came eventually to recommend for Scotland. It also voiced a common complaint: there were too many appointed bodies and independent boards administering Welsh affairs. One such body, the Development Corporation for Wales, a Welsh version of the Scottish Council (Development and Industry) which was set up in 1958 and is openly financed by the Welsh Office, saw things differently. It wanted to 'participate in the affairs of the [devolved Assembly]'. The Welsh teachers wanted to have education controlled by an all-Wales institution and the Welsh Schools Parents' Union agreed. The Welsh Counties Committee wanted for Wales whatever Scotland got.

The normally vociferous pressure groups, however, just as in Scotland, were silent. Perhaps they thought devolution would go away. After the publication in November 1975 of the Government's first definite proposals for creating a devolved Assembly – in the White Paper *Our Changing Democracy* – this hope could no longer be sustained. *Our Changing Democracy* proposed the creation of elected Assemblies for Scotland and Wales. The Scottish Assembly was to have legislative and executive powers; the Welsh Assembly, rather like a large local authority, was to have only executive authority. This proposal was definite and serious enough to provoke a response from many hitherto silent groups.

In general those pressure groups most comfortable when a Conservative government is in power were against devolution. The Scottish Office of the CBI, the Royal Bank of Scotland, the Committee of the Scottish Clearing Banks, the Glasgow Chamber of Commerce and the Dundee and Tayside Chamber of Commerce could not find a word between them in favour of the Government's proposals. The Scottish Landowners' Federation and the National Farmers' Union were in the same camp. The only pressure group associated with industry which favoured the government's proposals was the Scottish Council (Development and Industry). Having taken the view that overcentralisation of government was the most damaging force within the UK, it had little choice but to back the Government's radical proposals to deal with the problem.

The academic profession was divided just as it was in its evidence to Kilbrandon. The numerically larger teachers' unions and the students were for devolution but the Association of University Teachers and the Scottish University Courts were opposed. There was a tendency for the professions in general to mirror this pattern. The more senior and socially secure members of each profession were either opposed to devolution in principle, or agnostic about the principle but certain that they did not want to be devolved themselves. A division along these lines is perceivable in medicine and accountancy although not in the law. The Royal Colleges of Surgeons and of Physicians and the BMA were worried about 'the introduction of a politically biased tier' into the health service. The Pharmaceutical Society and the Society of Radiographers were for UK-wide standards in their work and hence against devolution. On the other hand, the Pharmaceutical General

Council (Scotland) and the British Association of Occupational Therapists (Scottish branch) had worries about the details of the proposals but were not opposed to being devolved.

The legal associations produced comprehensive and original, if negative, comments. They all pointed to the difficulties in the proposals. The Council of the Law Society and the Scottish Branch of the Chartered Institute of Public Finance and Accountancy emphasised the difficulties in the method (the block grant) by which the government was proposing to finance the new Assemblies.

The building industry was a world on its own. The Scottish Federation of Housing Associations, the Scottish Society of Directors of Planning, and the Royal Incorporation of Architects of Scotland, were unanimous in looking forward to working in a devolved Scotland. Perhaps this had something to do with the fact that most of their work was for local authorities and local authorities were going to be devolved. It made little sense for the building industry to be separate. Some people in this industry also felt that it suffered badly from the lack of parliamentary time at Westminster and that a devolved Assembly would have more time to look at the industry's problems. Amongst the professional groups in this industry only the Royal Institute of Chartered Surveyors were centralists. They were joined in this by the most anti-devolutionist of all the Scottish unions, the Union of Construction, Allied Trade and Technicians. The old centralist sympathy was also strong in the Electrical Trades Union, the Society of Graphical and Allied Trades and the Association of Scientific, Technical and Managerial Staffs.

In general, however, those pressure groups which normally support Labour governments supported the Government's plans for Scotland and Wales. The crucial unions here were the Transport and General Workers' Union the National Union of Mineworkers and the Amalgamated Union of Engineering Workers. The Government's White Paper was also welcomed by the local government union, the General and Municipal Workers Union and the Scottish Union of Bakers and Allied Workers. The Scottish and Welsh TUCs also came out in favour. By late 1975 the trade unions were certainly moving towards devolution, and they are amongst the most powerful pressure groups in the land. But those who did back devolution did so as late converts and it is difficult to believe that they cared deeply about the subject. Their conversion can be explained as an act of loyalty towards the Labour Party on what was clearly a political (as opposed to a trade union) issue. In the case of some unions (both pro- and anti-devolution) the impression is inescapable that a few dedicated and influential individuals were able to swing their less concerned colleagues. Alec Kitson, of the Transport & General Workers' Union had a powerful influence both in his union and through his union on the Labour Party. The Construction workers, on the other hand, were also dominated by a small group. For most trade unionists the main factor was the safety of their government, not the fate of the Union. Though the TUC's arch comments to Kilbrandon could no longer be made – some trade unions had debated the issue at their annual conferences – the essence of it remained true: the unions didn't really care.

The only groups which were consistently in favour of devolution were the purveyors of traditional cultural values – the churches, especially the established churches of Scotland and Wales, the cultural and language societies, the school teachers and the solicitors. These groups are dependably – in the politest possible way, of course – anti-English, for they fear anglicisation as the major threat to the continuance of their own culture. They are also not, although not for this reason, the heavyweights of the corporate state. This pattern makes sense of the apparent absence of the University teachers from the pro-devolution camp. The universities (in Scotland) have long been suspect as bastions of English influence, and very much resented for this reason. The University of Wales is similarly suspect.

Thus we see that the pressure for devolution did not come from the usually powerful pressure groups. They were either tepidly opposed (the CBI) or positively indifferent (the TUC to Kilbrandon), or tepidly committed (the TUC after 1974). These groups followed the debate, but they did not initiate it nor push it along. If devolution was going to make a return to more democratic, and less corporate, decision-making easier, this prospect has not seemed to trouble those who are expected to lose influence in the process. It is also worth recalling that public pressure for devolution was not intense. From the fact that most people say, when they are prompted, that they would like more power for their region, it has been deduced that they want devolved Assemblies on the lines proposed in the Kilbrandon Report and subsequently enacted by the Government. This is a shaky deduction. For the source of the pressure for devolution we must look elsewhere. We must look to those who convinced the party leaders to back devolution, and we must look to the debate within the parties themselves.

REFERENCES

1. Kilbrandon, 'Committee on the Constitution', *Research Papers No.* 7 p. 62 from Table 45.
2. BUTLER, D. and STOKES, D. *Political Change in Britain: The Evolution of Electoral Choice* 2nd edition (London: Macmillan, 1974), see p. 466; cited in full in Steed, M. 'Devolution: The English Dimension', *PSA Working Paper*, Sept. 1977, p. 23.
3. Kilbrandon, *Minute of Evidence* (UK) Vol. IX, para. 1, p. 95.
4. *Ibid*, para. 2, p. 95.
5. *Ibid*, (Scotland) Vol. IV, para. 4, p. 74.

Chapter seven

THE BRITISH PARTIES MANOEUVRE

British governments generally claim to stand for the whole country and to rule in the interests of the whole country. This claim has a double aspect: it is a doctrine about how the parties conduct themselves in government. They accept responsibility for the whole country, not just for the interests of their special group of voters. They also appeal for the votes of every – or nearly every – group in the society. They are 'catch-all' parties.

In the decades before the 1970s, Conservative governments found it easier to sustain this claim than did Labour governments. The Conservatives drew support in large numbers from every class in society. Nearly half their support regularly came from working-class electors. Labour, on the other hand, won only a very small proportion of its vote from the middle class. In this important respect the Conservative Party was more a national party than the Labour Party. Also, the Labour Party originally set itself up as the party of the working man, specifically of the trade union and labour movement. It had difficulty maintaining that it could at once be the party of a section of the country and at the same time the party of the whole country. In practice it tended to emphasise its role as the defender of the working class when it was in opposition and its role as party of responsible government when it was in power.

As long as the overwhelming majority of the electorate were content to vote for one or other of these parties, the battle between them could be conducted in terms of this kind. In 1951, when the two-party fight between the Labour and Conservative parties was at its most intense, 82.6 per cent of the population voted and 48.8 per cent of the voters cast their ballot for Labour while 48 per cent voted Conservative. In that year 0.7 per cent of the Welsh population voted for Plaid candidates (there were four) and 0.3 per cent of Scots voted for the two SNP candidates. But the two main parties lost their dominance, and increasing numbers of Welsh and Scots turned instead to the National party of their country. At the 1966 general election 75.8 per cent of the UK electorate voted; 48.1 per cent of them for Labour and 41.9 per cent for Conservative candidates. By this time the vote for the two National parties, though still small, could no longer be dismissed. 4.3 per cent of the Welsh and 5 per cent of Scots voted for the Nationalist party candidates (of which there were 20 and 23 respectively).

Immediately after this election the pull of the Nationalist parties came to be felt by the major parties for the first time. The first by-election after the 1966 general election was held in the Welsh seat of Carmarthen. Plaid's candidate was their President, Gwynfor Evans. He won with 39.0 per cent of the poll. This victory on 14 July 1966 transformed Welsh, Scottish and, to an extent not then dreamed of, British politics. Evans' victory set the Nationalist parties alight. He immediately became known as the member for Wales. He was not slow to use the House of Commons as a propaganda forum for his party and his country. In his first Parliament Evans tabled hundreds of parliamentary questions. Evans' victory was followed by hugely successful recruitment campaigns by Plaid, campaigns, which in their turn were to help the party fight the two subsequent by-elections at Rhondda West (9 March 1967) and Caerphilly (18 July 1968). In both these seats Plaid performed well. In Rhondda West it improved from a general election performance of 16.1 per cent of the vote to 46.7 per cent in the by-election; in Caerphilly it improved from 11.1 per cent to 40.4 per cent. In both cases overwhelming Labour majorities were cut to small leads. In both cases Labour had had a 60 per cent lead over its nearest rival (Plaid in the first seat, Conservative in the second) In Rhondda West its lead was cut to 2.3 per cent and in Caerphilly to 5.3 per cent.

Plaid's success in Wales was mirrored by the SNP in Scotland. The first Scottish by-election of the 1966 Parliament was in Glasgow Pollok. The Nationalist party had not even contested it in the general election, in which Labour had narrowly beaten the Conservatives. In the by-election also held on 9 March 1967 the SNP candidate won 30.0 per cent of the vote, having taken votes from both the major parties, but more from Labour so that the Conservatives won the seat. The effect of Glasgow Pollok on Scottish politics was very similar to Carmarthen's on Welsh politics. It electrified a hitherto somnolent polity. The National Party in Scotland, like its confederate in Wales, gained enormously in membership and prepared for the forthcoming local government elections – in which it did embarrassingly well – with glee. Pollok was a breakthrough for the SNP in another way: at Pollok, for the first time since the 1930s, the party was taken seriously by the press. They recognised the glamour in the National Party and promoted this glamour to the Scottish people. This press recognition helped the party to focus attention on its issues and its candidates in future elections. But the breakthrough came in November 1967. The SNP candidate, Mrs Winifred Ewing, won the by-election at Hamilton, formerly a safe Labour seat. Mrs Ewing won 46.0 per cent of the vote; her party had not even fielded a candidate there in the previous general election. Both the Labour and the Conservative parties lost votes; but Labour, which had counted on mining seats like Hamilton for a generation, was stunned.

These by-election triumphs, and the victories which occurred in 1967 and 1968 (the SNP's peak) in local government elections, at once showed that the Scottish and Welsh electors had changed, and signalled to the British parties that they had better change too, and fast, if they were to continue to claim to represent the nation. Scottish and Welsh electors were no longer voting for the parties of their grandfathers' choice. They were voting in very large numbers for parties which identified themselves primarily with a nation, not with a class. In the case of Plaid, this was a matter of identity with the nation first and the working class second; in the case of the Scottish National Party it was a matter (a more direct challenge to the old party alignment this) of nation first and class identification nowhere. The most important effect of the SNP victories, then, was on the British parties.

The position of the two great British parties was not identical. The Conservative Party was accustomed to being a minority in Wales. Before the Labour Party was even dreamt of, the Liberal Party had held a large majority of seats in Welsh parliamentary constituencies. Labour had replaced it as the majority party. Wales was more a one-party political system than a two-party system. Labour's greatest victory in Wales came, as it happens, only months before the Plaid broke through in Carmarthen: in the March 1966 general election Labour won 32 of the 36 seats. In Scotland it also achieved its highest total in the 1966 general election: 46 of the 71 seats. In 1966 the Conservative Party won 3 seats in Wales and 20 seats in Scotland.

The rise of the Nationalist parties was thus more immediately threatening to the Labour Party than to the Conservatives, but the most worrying threat was to the constitution. The parties are not simply the private vehicles of those who run them. They have a role in the constitution. As the rise of the National parties in Scotland and Wales has made clear, one of the roles of the parties has been to unite the United Kingdom. The fact that they could claim to speak for substantial proportions of the people of each of the British nations made it impossible for individual Nationalists, or the National parties of the non-English nations, to claim to represent their peoples. The job for the British parties, when the Nationalists had established themselves as serious electoral competitors, was at once to regain their own popularity and, thereby, to reassert the dominance of the United Kingdom in the non-English nations. They had to find some way of convincing the Scottish and Welsh people to vote for them again. In the circumstances of the late 1960s this was taken to mean they must learn to portray themselves convincingly to the people of Scotland and Wales as Scottish and Welsh. It would not be an easy task.

There is a paradox here: the more difficult the task the more necessary it is. The Conservative Party in Scotland grew weaker, as a political force in Scotland and as a part of the Conservative Party, when the Nationalists started to win its seats and its votes. Yet, it was precisely when the party was so weakened that it needed to fight hardest. Much the same was true of the Labour Party. The party that failed to hold Hamilton in the 1967 by-election needed to rebuild all over Scotland. This local weakness in the face of the rising SNP – and for Labour in Wales, the rising Plaid – points to the reason why the decision to commit the British parties to devolution came eventually from the (English) centres of the parties. The local branches were too weak or too shocked – or too deferential to London – to make the commitment.

The Labour Party in Wales provided a vivid example of the problem.[1] It had been committed to measures of further devolution since 1965. The position was then hardened to what was to be its high point when the Welsh party prepared its evidence for the Kilbrandon Commission. The process began with the preparation of evidence by the Welsh Council of the Labour Party in 1969. A research group within the Welsh party had proposed a commitment to an elected Assembly with control over the domestic functions which the Kilbrandon Commission was to propose: housing, roads, health, education, local government, regional planning, police and fire services, environmental services, tourism, cultural and rural amenities and forestry. The proposal was for a directly elected Assembly which would have legislative and executive control over these functions with the right to raise taxes on them, serviced by its own civil service. The Labour Party in London was strongly opposed to these ideas. Though it had no formal power to force the Welsh Party to see things its way, members of political parties do not like public disagreements.

(Transport House tried to persuade all constituency parties not to give evidence to Kilbrandon and a circular letter to this effect was sent out. There were no sanctions, but only one constituency party gave evidence). The Welsh Labour Party backed down on all its demands but one. It proposed a directly elected Assembly to Kilbrandon. Even then, it needed to fight for approval to make this demand. The Welsh Labour Party has not again gone beyond the position fought out on this occasion, though it did try, but the Welsh TUC was not so easily dissuaded from backing a legislative assembly for Wales. Not for the last time the Labour Party in Wales made policy for Wales with cloth cut to a Westminster pattern.

Another of Labour's problems was that its Scottish organisation was opposed to the creation of an elected Assembly in Scotland to handle Scottish Affairs. The Labour Party had been committed to devolution until 1958. From 1958 until 1974 Labour in Scotland was a centralist party. In Scotland, moreover, the party was led by the Prime Minister's good friend and colleague, Mr William Ross, then MP for Kilmarnock. Mr Ross did not enjoy good relations with the press. He was too dour and school-masterly for their taste. The press did not like being lectured by the Secretary of State. In addition to the hostility which this personal conflict caused, Ross cultivated his reputation as the 'hammer of the Nats'. He used to call the SNP the 'Scots Narks'. Ross was convinced that Scotland was better off with the administrative devolution which he and preceding Scottish Secretaries had succeeded in winning from Whitehall than it would be if Scotland went it alone. His point was that with seventy-one MPs and a member of the British Cabinet the Scots were well looked after. If they traded these advantages for an elected Assembly in Edinburgh they would be weaker where it mattered – in the centre of power in Westminster and Whitehall.

Thus, Labour's original response to the rise of the SNP in 1966, 1967 and 1968 was one of horror and contempt. Labour was horrified because it knew that it depended on winning a majority of Scottish seats to have any hope of winning an overall majority at Westminster. The party had also become accustomed to thinking of itself as the political voice of Scotland and did not take kindly to being displaced from that role. Labour also realised that it was in a poor position to fight back: never rich in individual members, the party was at a low point in the mid-1960s. In some safe Labour seats the party had ceased to function at all. Originally, the rise of the SNP led the Labour Party to react against everything the SNP demanded and, since the SNP was then a devolution party (it became committed to devolution in 1962),

Labour's centralism was reinforced. Even so, the small band of remaining devolutionists within the Labour Party in Scotland saw that the rise of the SNP might be used to their advantage. They could try to persuade their party to embrace devolution as a way of heading off the Nationalists' ultimate demand for complete independence. At the 1968 Scottish Council Conference the Hillhead (Glasgow) Constituency Party moved a resolution in favour of a Scottish Parliament. It received derisory support. In the 1969 Conference, the Leith (Edinburgh) Constituency Party asked for a Speaker's Conference to consider the problem. The motion was remitted to the Executive (normally a procedural way of dealing with a proposal the executive could but does not want to defeat).

There was no question of the Labour Party in Scotland (or the Conservative Party for that matter) pleading with its headquarters in London to grant a concession to Scotland. On the contrary, if the decision had been left to the Scottish sections of either party it is doubtful if either would have been committed to devolution even today. The Scottish party was not even consulted.

Richard Crossman reveals in his *Diaries* that both Harold Wilson and Edward Heath took the Nationalist threat very seriously and both thought something had to be done about it. On 5 May 1967 he reflected that: 'The PM [i.e. Wilson] has several times said that the question of decentralisation and regional government – Welsh Nationalism, Scottish Nationalism – might become the most explosive issue at the next election.' In November, on the night of Mrs Ewing's triumph in Hamilton, he remembered, 'I was reminded of how Ted Heath had said last week at the Broadcasting Committee hearing that Nationalism is the biggest single factor in our politics today.' This pressure forced ministers like Crossman to overcome their contempt for the non-English and their ministers. On 12 June 1967 he noted:

As I've recorded before, there are a number of Welsh MPs – headed by the present Secretary of State, Cledwyn Hughes – who regard the threat of Welsh nationalism as very serious and would like to meet it by moving towards something very like Welsh self-government. They are, of course, opposed by most of the South Wales MPs, since the miners don't in the least want a Welsh Parliament and think any surrender to the nationalists is an act of cowardly appeasement. Their conviction that Wales does better economically as part of Britain is almost certainly true. But so too is the conviction of the MPs from North Wales that Welsh nationalism is a force to be reckoned with. . . . Now here was Cledwyn Hughes back again with his miserable recommendation for a co-opted Welsh Council, which as far as I could see would do nothing but supervise tourism. Barbara Castle, I'm glad to say, supported me when I said that it was no good attacking Cledwyn since he was faced with a very real political difficulty. He had to move forward far enough to hold his position.[2]

For his part, the Conservative leader, Edward Heath, was anxious that his party should do something to improve its attractiveness to Scottish voters. His problem was considerable. It was not so long ago, in 1955, that the Conservative Party had won a majority (50.1 per cent) of Scottish votes at a general election. At that election the Conservatives won 36 seats in Scotland to the Labour Party's 34; the Liberals won 1. Yet the Conservatives' position had been slipping steadily since the 1955 election. In 1959 Scotland had swung to the Labour Party, against the British trend. In the 1966 general election the Labour Party had captured 46 seats to the Conservatives' 20. The Liberals had won 5. Yet it was not inconceivable that the party could do something to reverse its recent bad fortunes and recoup the ground it had lost in the past three elections. Heath's reaction was to commit his party to devolution.

In order to do this he came to his Scottish Party's annual conference in Perth in 1968 and announced his conversion to devolution at the rally which the party normally holds after the conference is closed. Heath informed his party that they were a Scottish party and had to be committed to Scottish causes. Therefore he was appointing a committee under the Chairmanship of Sir Alec Douglas Home who would advise the party on what form of devolution to embrace.

The Home Commission reported before the 1970 general election and the substance of its proposals was embodied in the party's 1970 general election manifesto. The Home Commission recommended the creation in Edinburgh of a directly elected Assembly to be called 'the Scottish Convention'. It would perform the tasks previously performed by the Scottish Grand Committee – i.e., it would take the committee stage of Scottish legislation as that legislation was being enacted by the House of Commons. It would also take over the functions performed by the Standing Committee on Scottish Affairs; that is, it would have the right to examine Scottish Ministers on the performance of their tasks. Home also argued that his Convention would 'provide a focus for the discussion in public of Scottish affairs'. Two members of the Home Commission objected to the proposals on the grounds that there would be so little Scottish legislation for the proposed Convention to consider that it would spend most of its time looking for things to do and creating trouble.

The Home proposals did at least avoid many of the defects later ascribed to the Labour Government's Bill. Since the Scottish

Convention would only be the equivalent of a committee of the House of Commons, it could not initiate legislation. Moreover, if an SNP or Labour majority in the Convention should change legislation sent to it in a way which was completely unacceptable to a Conservative majority in the House of Commons, the latter could drop the Bill and thereby blame the Convention for preventing the passage of necessary legislation; or they could delete any troublesome amendments inserted by the Convention when the Bill went through its further stages in the House of Commons. Since the House of Commons would retain all its present power over Scottish legislation, there could be no case for reducing the number of Scottish MPs or for depriving the Secretary of State for Scotland of his seat in the British Cabinet. The Commission hoped that these features would make its proposals acceptable to English Conservatives and as well to Scottish devolutionists. It is worth noting that the Conservative Commision did not recommend any devolution to Wales. The Commission recognised that the pressure for change was coming from Scotland.

The Conservatives went in the 1970 election with a manifesto pledge which read:

Scotland, with its distinct identity, traditions and legal system, is particularly conscious of these problems. The Report of the Committee set up under Sir Alec Douglas Home offers a new chance for the Scottish people to have a greater say in their own affairs. Its contents, including the proposal for a Scottish Convention sitting in Edinburgh, will form a basis for the proposals we will place before Parliament, taking account of the impending re-organisation of local government.[3]

The Heath administration (June 1970 to February 1974) in fact did nothing about devolution. It had other priorities. It took Britain into the EEC, it reformed the law on trade union practices and it tried to bring peace to Northern Ireland. The reasons why devolution – and the problem of Scotland and Wales – were a low priority for their administration are not hard to find. The Nationalist parties of both Scotland and Wales had performed too poorly in the 1970 general election to frighten the British parties: with 11.4 per cent of the Scots vote the SNP won only one seat (the Western Isles) and with 11.5 per cent of the vote in Wales the Plaid won nothing. It was not until the end of the parliament that the Nationalist parties' fortunes recovered sufficiently for the British parties to take them seriously again. In November 1973 the SNP captured Glasgow Govan from Labour with the ebullient Mrs Margo MacDonald – but by this time the Conservative Government's fight with the miners which was to lead to the general election the following February was already under way. In this period the Labour Party in Wales was committed to a form of devolution for that country, the Labour Party in Scotland was not committed to devolution at all and the Conservative Party was committed to a form of devolution for Scotland, but not for Wales. It was during this period that the Kilbrandon commissioners sat.

REFERENCES

1. We are indebted to John Osmond for much help in preparing this part of the book. His book *Creative Conflict: The Politics of Welsh Devolution* (London: Routledge and Kegan Paul, 1978) especially pp. 180–189 contains a fuller account of these matters.
2. CROSSMAN, R. H. S. *The Diaries of a Cabinet Minister: Volume II. Lord President of the Council and Leader of the House of Commons 1966–68* (London: Hamish Hamilton and Jonathan Cape, 1976), p. 377.
3. 1970 Conservative party manifesto cited in CRAIG, F.W.S. *British General Election Manifestos 1900–1974* (London: Macmillan, 1975), p. 340.

Chapter eight
THE GOVERNMENT REACTS

The Kilbrandon Commission presented its report in October 1973. The Labour Government presented its first Bill on devolution, which contained a version of the ideas proposed by Kilbrandon, to the House of Commons on 29 November 1976. Two subsequent Bills embodying slightly amended versions of the original proposals, one for Scotland, the other for Wales, completed all their parliamentary stages in July 1978. In the period between the presentation of the Kilbrandon Report and the publication of the Government's first Bill, the battle over devolution took place mainly, though by no means entirely, within the Labour Party and between the Labour Cabinet and its civil service. Both these battles took place in private and important detail remains secret, although much of the substance of the debate can be discerned. In the period between the presentation of the Government's first Bill on devolution and its eventual success in getting Parliament to pass the amended successors to that Bill, the fight took place more or less openly on the floor of the House of Commons and in the country. As the two battles were quite different we will describe them in separate chapters. This chapter describes the movement from the Kilbrandon Report to the first Bill.

The general election of February 1974 resulted, to nearly universal surprise, in the return of a Labour government. The new Government had only a minority of seats, however, and everyone knew that a further general election would have to be held soon, probably within the year. This freak circumstance of two general elections close to one another, with the SNP in Scotland poised to win large numbers of additional seats from both the Labour and the Conservative parties, led both these parties to harden their commitments to devolution. In the February 1974 election the SNP had captured 21.9 per cent of the Scottish vote and ended with 7 MPs; 5 of them had won their seats from Conservatives. In Wales, on the other hand, Plaid Cymru had managed to win only 10.7 per cent of the votes and was still fourth. It won two seats.

One of the five Conservative MPs who lost to the SNP was the former Secretary of State for Scotland, Mr Gordon Campbell. It was a defeat of awesome proportions. Mr Campbell actually succeeded in raising his vote over his 1970 total, but Mrs Winnie Ewing, the one-time victor of Hamilton, captured his seat, Moray and Nairn, for the SNP because Labour voters moved over to her *en masse*. Scottish Conservatives could see that tactical voting of this kind would leave them few seats if repeated all over Scotland. More important for the devolution debate within the Conservative Party was the fact that Campbell was replaced as Scottish Conservative front-bench spokesman by Mr Alick Buchanan-Smith, who was a strong pro-devolutionist. The Conservative Conference in Ayr in May 1974 accepted its new spokesman's advice and voted to commit itself to an indirectly elected Assembly. The members of the new Assembly would be chosen from the newly created Scottish local authorities. This compromise pleased nobody. The October 1974 Conservative manifesto, however, followed its Scottish party's decision. It promised to create an Assembly whose members would be initially chosen from the local authorities. After the election – which the Labour Party won – the party set up a committee under Mr Malcolm Rifkind MP, which recommended a directly elected assembly to take second reading and Committee stages of Scottish Bills. This proposal was close to the Home Committee's ideas.

What was happening meanwhile within the SNP and Plaid? Since the votes and parliamentary seats won by the SNP and Plaid had been crucial in forcing the British parties to give serious consideration to setting up devolved legislatures in Edinburgh and Cardiff, these parties might reasonably have been expected to affect the course of the debate after February 1974 as well. Perhaps the most astonishing aspect of the politics of devolution and nationalism is that they did not. We have an almost complete bifurcation between politics within Scotland and Wales, which, as we have seen in the first part of this book produced strong nationalist political challenges, and politics at Westminster. Once devolution came to the centre of the stage in London, the Nationalist parties mattered hardly at all. For all their success at producing political machines which could harvest votes, the Nationalists did not produce impressive Westminster groups. And despite the eminently exploitable weaknesses of Labour's minority governments, the small National parties were not up to exerting much influence: Parnell had no emulator, either in tactical genius or following.

The real battle was within the Labour Party and most, but not all of that, was about the Labour Party in Scotland. Labour's hold on the majority of Scottish and Welsh seats and the vulnerability of her seats to further Nationalist advances produced sufficient anxiety to stir the party. Labour had fought the first 1974 election without any commitment to devolution. The party's election manifesto did not mention the subject. The first commitment by the Labour Party came in Harold Wilson's speech in defence of the Government's promises in the Queen's Speech. Tam Dalyell MP subsequently to be an arch opponent of devolution, described what happened:

The Queen's Speech, delivered on 12 March 1974, merely stated,

'My Ministers and I will initiate discussion in Scotland ... and bring forward proposals for consideration.' Harmless enough.

Lo and behold, that very same afternoon of 12th March, the Prime Minister, making his formal speech in which he explained the Government's measures to the House of Commons, referred to 'our intended discussions'. Interrupted by a somewhat cantankerous Mrs Ewing, demanding 'proposals instead of discussions', Mr. Wilson replied: 'We on this side believe in full consultation and discussions. We are not an authoritarian party. Of course, we shall publish a White Paper and a Bill' ... This was news indeed ... there had been no formal discussion within the Labour Party ... The damage was done ... From that moment, however, the pressures were on to bring the Labour Party, and particularly the Labour Party in Scotland, into line.[1]

Just how far the Labour Party in Scotland had to go before it could be brought into line was made clear that same day.

In preparation for the annual conference of the Scottish Council of the Labour Party (SCLP), the Executive Committee of that body issued a statement on 12 March which noted:

We welcome Kilbrandon's emphatic rejection of the Nationalist case. We do, however, accept that there is a real need to ensure that decisions affecting Scotland are taken in Scotland wherever possible.[2]

That this statement hardly signalled a wholehearted commitment to devolution goes without saying. The statement did not really commit the executive of the SCLP to anything more than the present Scottish Office structure. The difficulty was that the executive contained a good many members who were still strongly opposed to the concept of an elected Assembly. But the statement was so vague that the next day the Prime Minister could appoint his friend Lord Crowther-Hunt to advise ministers on devolution without being seen to be entirely out of step with the Scottish section of his party. Downing Street's announcement was nicely phrased. Crowther-Hunt was to give advice 'in connection with the work the government are putting in hand on the recommendations of the majority and minority reports of the Commission on the Constitution'.

Pro-devolutionists took heart from Wilson's choice of Crowther-Hunt. They would have been less happy if they had known that Mr Heath had secretly asked the Privy Council Office to get to work on the Kilbrandon proposals immediately after the publication of the report. There were already five groups of civil servants within the Privy Council Office working on devolution. They were (a) a constitutional arrangement group (which included the secretariat of the Kilbrandon Commission), (b) an executive devolution group, (c) a social services group, (d) a finance group, and (e) a trade and industry group. Thus, when Crowther-Hunt started he was taking over a project whose design, if not complete, was already sketched out and bore a strong resemblance to the prototype in the majority report, not the more devolutionist minority report. Crowther-Hunt succeeded in persuading civil servants in the Privy Council Office to consider the proposals of the minority report as well, but it was too late to make much difference.

Two weeks after the appointment of Crowther-Hunt, the Scottish Council of the Labour Party met for its annual conference and approved its Executive Committee's statement. But at this conference the SCLP was faced with a variety of propositions on devolution. There was a resolution hostile to devolution which had been proposed by the General and Municipal Workers' Union and seconded by Paisley Constituency Labour Party, as well as a number of resolutions which went well beyond the executive's cautious statement in favour of devolution. The conference heavily defeated the GMWU-Paisley resolution. On the other hand, the pro-devolutionists did not get the support from the large unions which they expected. Two pro-devolution members of the executive, Donald Dewar and John Pollock, convinced them that the executive was moving towards devolution and so there was no need to push them. The conference resolution was hardly good enough for the pro-devolutionists, and it seems likely they would have pushed their case harder, had they known how finely balanced the argument was on the executive. The pro-devolutionists contented themselves with putting more pressure on London.

Meanwhile the Welsh Council of the Labour Party (WCLP) was keeping up the pressure for a greater measure of devolution:[3] spurred into action by the even stronger demands of the WTUC, its executive published a statement in April which proposed that a Welsh Assembly should have some formal way of influencing legislation for Wales. It also asked that the Assembly be set up in a way which would enable it to grow into more responsibility and power with the passage of time. The statement was made in preparation for the party's annual conference. When this met in May, there was vigorous conflict, especially between the South Wales Union of Mineworkers and the more moderate Swansea Labour Association. The miners wanted a full legislative chamber to be set up straight away. It has been suggested that a card vote would have led to an easy victory for the miners and the other pro-devolutionist unions. The platform, however, succeeded in avoiding a vote. It argued that any decision would embarrass the Government, which, it was known, was about to produce a White Paper on devolution. Thus, for the second time, pro-devolutionists within the Labour Party backed down.

On 3 June the Government produced its first White Paper on devolution, *Devolution within the United Kingdom – Some Alternatives for Discussion*, which contained a series of speculative propositions and asked for comment. Two things about this White Paper appear to have been more a public relations exercise than a serious consultative document. Firstly, the Government normally allows a reasonable time for interested parties to respond to its plans, yet this White Paper was succeeded in three months by another in which the Government put forward its own ideas. Second, the White Paper was noteworthy in consisting of a series of alternatives, whereas White Papers usually contain definite proposals, and in the recent past have often been tantamount to a proposal to legislate. (This June 1974 White Paper was so tentative that it did not even obtain the dignity of a Command Number). *Devolution within the United Kingdom: Some Alternatives for Discussion* listed the alternative suggestions for devolution which had been commended by members of the Kilbrandon Commission. These were lettered from 'A' to 'G'. 'A' was a schematic version of the majority report, 'B' was the minority report, and so on. Thus, the publication of the White Paper committed the Government to nothing, but it did formally redeem the Prime Minister's pledge of 12 March. Had the Government been forced to call an election shortly thereafter, this might have been important. But there was certainly no reason why the Welsh Labour Party needed to put off making up its mind in advance of the White Paper.

Since scheme 'A' of the White Paper (its version of the Kilbrandon majority report) formed the basis of the Government's subsequent proposals, one or two features of this scheme are of interest. One point concerns taxation. The White Paper noted:

Two crucial economic issues stand out for discussion. One is whether in the area of taxation and public expenditure enough powers could be devolved to Scotland and Wales to enable Scottish and Welsh governments to make full use of the other powers which the major schemes theoretically give them, while at the same time leaving the United Kingdom Government with fully adequate economic and financial powers to cope with the problems of demand management and the balance of payments . . .[4]

This linkage of the problem of taxation to the problem of allowing the Scottish and Welsh governments to 'make full use of the other powers' granted to them is, of course, quite right – a government without the power to tax is hardly a government at all. Another interesting point is the willingness of the UK Government, in this White Paper, to speak of the devolved legislatures as *governments*. Later on, it became quite touchy about how that word was used. Thirdly, it is worth noting here that the Government was still thinking of treating Scotland and Wales similarly. Fourthly, Scheme 'A' spoke of developing certain 'subjects' (this is the word Kilbrandon used too; we have referred to 'functions') and allowing the Assemblies to inherit the legislation of these functions already passed at Westminster. In the event, the Government did propose to devolve subjects but defined them by reference to existing legislation. In other words, the Scottish Assembly would not be given power to legislate on 'housing' but rather, power to legislate on 'housing, within the terms of the Housing (Scotland) Act of . . .' This method of defining the devolved powers draws the net around the Assembly's competence more sharply. Finally, scheme 'A' noted that the Scottish and Welsh Assembles would have their own civil servants, which would be separate from the Westminster civil service.

At this point, the SCLP executive threw a wrench into the devolution machine. Meeting on 2 June with only eleven of its twenty-nine members present (Scotland was playing football in the World Cup that afternoon), the executive considered its response to the White Paper. Ron Hayward, General Secretary of the Labour Party, had written to the Scottish executive urging it to accept the Government's plans. Unmoved by this, or the urgings of NEC member John Forrester of the AUEW, the eleven members of the EC voted by 6 votes to 5 against all the proffered alternatives. On the following Monday morning, the *Daily Record* published the names on both sides. Tom Fulton, Donald Dewar, Hugh Brown, George Robertson and Frank Gormill had voted for devolution. They were outnumbered by Sadie Hatton, David Davidson, Jean McVey, Geoff Shaw, Allan Campbell McLean and Peter Talbot.

On the same day, there was a meeting of the Welsh Labour Party executive. It did not know what was happening in Glasgow. It accepted the Welsh TUC line that more economic power should be devolved to Wales. Instead of urging economic power for the Assembly – largely out of fear of putting the Scots on the spot as being too laggard – they urged the creation of a Welsh Development Agency in the Welsh Office. They put their finger, at this meeting, on one of the greatest weaknesses in the political case for devolution. If Scots and Welsh voters were voting for the National parties of their countries because they were fed up with the economic performance of the British Government, the British Government was responding by offering them control over all manner of domestic affairs, *except* economic life. The Welsh meeting went almost completely unnoticed in the uproar that greeted the Scots' decision.

The London centre of the Labour Party was enraged by what its Scottish Council had done. Unless the '6–5' decision were reversed, it would be impossible for the Government to publish a serious White Paper on devolution, and without that they would be naked to the Nationalists' threat at the forthcoming general election. At the next meeting of the National Executive (NEC) of the Labour Party on 26 June, two of the Scottish members, Alex Kitson of the TGWU and Judith Hart, MP for North Lanark, demanded that the NEC order the executive of the Scottish Party to call an emergency conference to reverse its '6–5' decision, To this end, the Scottish Organiser of the Labour Party, Peter Allison (who was paid for and appointed by Transport House, Labour's London headquarters), was called to London and told to hold the special conference. At the next meeting of the executive of the SCLP on 8 July, the Scots agreed to do as they were told.

They were helped to see that their decision had to be changed by a 'private' Labour Party poll which had been leaked to the press. The poll had been conducted by Market and Opinion Research Incorporated (MORI) – the company Labour often retains to do its polls at general election time. This MORI poll showed that Labour would lose thirteen seats in Scotland to the Nationalists, were it not to change its devolution policy. Politicians do not need to be given that sort of information twice. At a meeting on 25 July, the NEC – also, as it happens, with barely a dozen members present – agreed to a motion from Alec Kitson that it declare its support for devolution publicly. This decision, taken at the end of the meeting, risked a public split with the Scottish Party. But it also increased the pressure on the party to change its mind.

The Special Conference was held on 16 August in the Co-operative

Halls, Dalintober Street, Glasgow. The devolutionists won a victory there that few in their hearts really wanted. The large trade unions' block votes were delivered without enthusiasm. The key proposition before the delegates was No. 4. It stated:

That this Conference, recognising the desire of the Scottish people for a greater say in the running of their own affairs, calls for the setting up of a directly elected Assembly with legislative powers within the context of the political and economic unity of the UK.[5]

It was carried overwhelmingly. The conference also called for the retention by Scotland of its existing constitutional advantages, seventy-one MPs and a Secretary of State within the Cabinet. This decision was a bitter blow to the Welsh. The SCLP had not only reversed the '6-5' decision, but had gone on to demand the legislative powers, which the Welsh had refrained from demanding so as not to embarrass the Scots. It was a bitter pill for both the Welsh party and the Welsh TUC. Now they could hardly argue for legislative powers or equality with the Scots because their own documents had asked for less. The devolutionists within the Welsh Labour Party have never regained the initiative. In Scotland the effect was the opposite. Soon it was difficult to remember that the Labour Party had once opposed devolution. Indeed, Mr Ross told the party at its 1977 annual conference that it had always backed devolution. The argument within the party became not 'whether' but 'how much' and the pressure was always for 'more'.

The following Wednesday, 21 August, a sub-committee of the Labour Party's National Executive met and decided to put the proposals of the Welsh and Scottish parties into a paper. This paper, called *Bringing Power to the People*, was published with the authority of the party's powerful Home Policy Committee on 5 September. The party committed itself, and seemingly its Government, on what all knew to be the eve of a general election, to creating directly elected assemblies in Scotland and Wales. These assemblies would be financed by block grants. The Scottish Assembly would have legislative powers. As it happened, the party committed the Cabinet in a way it could not appreciate. The Cabinet was also meeting on 5 September and had before it a paper drawn up by the constitution unit of the Privy Council Office (under Gerry Fowler MP) which proposed substantially less devolution than *Bringing Power to the People*. When the discrepancy was noticed, the Cabinet realised it had no choice but to back the paper just then being published by the party. In this way, for once, the party outmanoeuvred the civil servants.

Twelve days later the Government issued its second White Paper, an earlier version of which had been considered by the Cabinet on 5 September. This new White Paper was called *Democracy and Devolution: Proposals for Scotland and Wales* (Cmnd. 5732). The White Paper began, somewhat defensively, by pointing to the existing administrative devolution to both Scotland and Wales. It admitted that not much had been done for England to date, but promised to look into proposals to democratise some features of English government. It was noticeable that the White Paper claimed that the existing system had served the Scottish people particularly well. They were enjoying a level of public expenditure per head very significantly higher than the rest of Britain. No such benefit was claimed for the newer and smaller administrative system of Wales. It went on to propose the creation of something very like Scheme 'A', save that the Welsh Assembly would have no legislative powers, and that the Government had discovered a difficulty in devolving any right to raise revenue to the new Assemblies. Instead, both would be financed by block grants. Nothing was said about whether the assemblies were to be served by separate civil services.

In a three-paragraph section towards the end of the White Paper, the Government acknowledged the relevance of off-shore oil to devolution. The intention to establish Scottish and Welsh Development Agencies was stressed. The Government's unease on this issue was clear. Everyone knew that the Scottish National Party would be making an issue of the oil revenues in the forthcoming election so the government could not afford to say nothing. But it was determined to keep central control of the oil revenues. The White Paper asserted that these revenues should be wisely used for the benefit of all. These paragraphs about oil, the granting of legislative powers to the Scottish Assembly, but not to the Welsh, and the stress placed at the beginning of the Paper on the benefit the Scottish people had already received from the Westminster system, pointed to the Government's increasing conviction that the politics of devolution and nationalism had really become the politics of Scottish devolution and nationalism. The Scots had the oil, a buoyant Nationalist Party and a better developed administrative system. The battle would be fought in Scotland; Wales had become a minor front. The day after the White Paper *Democracy and Devolution: Proposals for Scotland and Wales* was published, 18 September, the Prime Minister called a general election for October.

We have already emphasised the way in which the commitment of the Labour Party was made from the centre and forced on the periphery (particularly the Scots) and have noticed the important way in which the Assemblies proposed were irrelevant to the ailments of Scotland and Wales. It is perhaps also worth noticing the way the conjunction of the two elections and the fact of further gains by the SNP served to politicise the issue. Because so much was at stake for the Government, and because another general election was imminent, the decisions on devolution throughout this period were made to a remarkable extent by the party and not by the civil service. When it came, after the October election, to planning the precise form of the elected assemblies, the precedence was reversed: the civil service made the running and the party lagged behind. The latter is the more usual relationship between the two in contemporary British politics. For eight months, eight important months in the politics of devolution and nationalism, the politicians held the cards and made the decisions.

Labour's manifesto for the October 1974 election promised that 'the next Labour government will create elected assemblies in Scotland and Wales'. The party's manifesto for Scotland promised that the newly created Scottish Development Agency would be responsible to the Secretary of State. It did not promise to devolve control of the Scottish Development Agency. The same was true in Wales of the Welsh Development Agency.

The effect of the election – which resulted in a Labour Government with a small majority of seats – was to confirm the direction of the devolution argument. In Wales, the election over, the devolutionists fell back even more. Although Plaid did pick up one more seat, they won fewer votes and remained the fourth party. In Scotland, the election had the opposite effect. The SNP emerged as the second party in votes, having displaced the Conservative Party and it won four additional seats – all from the Conservatives. But most important of all for the Labour Party, now firmly in government, the SNP came second to Labour in 35 of Labour's 41 Scottish seats. This result convinced many in Scotland that the SNP was poised to become the majority party in Scotland at the next General Election: Labour had held 41 of the 71 seats with 36 per cent of the vote. The SNP had 30 per cent of the vote. It seemed that with only a small additional increase, this apparently unstoppable machine would gain a majority of seats. The politically conscious press, especially the *Scotsman*, was not slow to take the point. It hired more political staff and set about making itself the paper of devolution. For many weeks after the October 1974 election, devolution was hardly ever off the front page. There can be no doubt that this attention helped the devolutionists by keeping their issue on the boil in Scotland.

The divergence between the mood of the Welsh and Scottish wings of the Labour Party was evident at their 1975 conferences. The Scottish party's conference only narrowly failed to pass a resolution, tabled by the TGWU, which called upon the government:

(1) to ensure that the Assembly, headed by an executive body, has a guaranteed basis of finance and revenue raising powers. (2) to consider devolving to the Assembly, Department of Trade and Industry functions relating to the development of existing industry and attraction of new industry to Scotland. (3) to make the SDA answerable to the Assembly. (4) in conjunction with the Manpower Services Commission and the training services agency, to develop further labour recruitment and training programmes consistent with the needs of existing and developing industry.[6]

Harry Ewing MP (Falkirk and Stirling Burghs), then Scottish Minister with responsibility for devolution, pleaded with the conference to pass the motion if it wanted to have a say. The Whitehall machine was closing in and this was the last chance for the Scottish party to make its feelings known. When the resolution was lost by 353,000 votes to 341,000, it was reckoned a big defeat for the devolutionists. Less than a year before the party had been tripped up by the '6–5' decision. Now it had only just failed to demand more devolution than the Government was offering.

The March 1975 decision may have been reckoned a defeat for the pro-devolutionists by even stronger supporters of devolution in the press and the SNP, but this reckoning only served to disguise how far the party had come. We notice here the first glimmerings of an error which came (in 1978 and 1979) seriously to mislead the pro-devolutionists in the SNP. Because these pro-devolutionists always wanted 'more' they failed to appreciate how far Labour had travelled in their direction. Thus they failed to realise how the Labour Party was narrowing the popular support which the 'maximalists' could command. Devolution commanded majority assent; independence did not. Secondly, eventually more crucially, the pro-devolutionists were so amazed by the clumsiness of Scottish Labour's move to devolution that they failed to grasp Labour's underlying resolve to fulfil its new commitments. Labour in Scotland was slowly outmanoeuvring the maximalist devolutionists and the SNP. The SNP's leadership was not to wake up to this fact until it was too late.

Meanwhile at the conference of the Welsh Council of the Labour Party, the anti-devolutionists grasped the initiative. Led by Leo Abse MP (Pontypool), Don Anderson MP (Swansea East) Neil Kinnock MP (Bedwellty) and Fred Evans MP (Caerphilly), they argued for a commitment by the party to a referendum on devolution. The campaign for a referendum was not to be carried within the WCLP in either 1975 or 1976 (though the Government did concede the idea in early 1977), largely because the WTUC wouldn't hear of it. This loss of heart by the Welsh Labour Party opened the way for Plaid to regain the devolutionist initiative in Wales. They were able to play on the feeling in Wales that what was good enough for Scotland was good enough for Wales too.

While this debate was going on within its party, the Government was making its detailed plans. It put to use the committees (and some of the thinking) which it had inherited from the Conservative Government. Mr Heath had set up a committee structure to consider the proposals of the Kilbrandon commission. The key body within this structure was the Constitution Unit, which was a part of the Privy Council Office. The minister responsible for it was the Lord President of the Council. While Mr Wilson was Prime Minister, the Lord President was Edward Short MP (now Lord Glenamarra), and during Mr Callaghan's Premiership, the Lord President was Michael Foot. When Mr Wilson first returned to office in March 1974, he asked his old friend, Lord Crowther-Hunt, to be his constitutional adviser and as such he joined in these deliberations as a member of the Constitution Unit.

The Constitution Unit wrote to the various ministries asking them, once it had been decided to devolve power, what powers they currently had which they could do without and pass on to departments responsible to the devolved Assemblies. This was not a strong request. No civil servant ever wants to give up control over anything; being human, they are not likely to want to reduce their own powers. Since much of the work of the civil service involves harmonising standards around the country, it would have been surprising if they had taken kindly to the notion that the work they were doing could be better done henceforth if it were divided between three sections, one each for Scotland, Wales and England. Those Scottish and Welsh Office civil servants who received this request from the Constitution Unit were, of course, in a different position from those in the British ministries. For them, there was no question of keeping control uniform throughout Britain. Rather, it was a matter of either keeping responsibilities within British ministries operating in Scotland or Wales or allowing them to go to departments answerable to elected Assemblies.

The typical Whitehall method of decision-making weighted the scales against extensive devolution. There was no question of reaching a 'rational' decision (for the very good reason that no one knew what 'rationality' dictated). Instead, the pressure was always to reach an accommodation between the various interests represented round a table. This meant that the largest number of interests prevailed. Thus, within the civil service service machinery itself, the British ministries were always likely to prevail over the Scottish and Welsh Offices – even when those two offices worked together – just because there would always be seven or eight civil servants from British ministries on any particular committee for each Scottish and Welsh Office civil servant. No matter how well the Scottish and Welsh Office civil servants urged the case for Scotland and Wales (which in this context meant the case for more devolution) they were always outnumbered and that meant out-argued.

The structure of decision-making made it difficult for political control to be reasserted once the Constitution Unit had collected its information and made its recommendations. The Unit reported its ideas to a committee of Permanent secretaries. These top-ranking civil servants in turn reported their conclusions to the Cabinet. The Cabinet may, of course, change any proposals put to it. But it would have been difficult at this stage and with such a major and complicated measure to rearrange the complex series of proposals. To be sure there was an informal group of concerned politicians: Mr Edward Short, (who alone among them was in the Cabinet) Lord Crowther-Hunt, Mr Gerry Fowler and Mr Harry Ewing. This group might have been able to affect the course of decision-making, but, as far as we can tell, they were not, on the whole, taken terribly seriously. Furthermore, with no disrespect to the ministers, the permanent secretaries had been around Whitehall for some time, knew what they wanted, and how Whitehall operated.

Much of this manoeuvring took place between the October 1974 election and March 1975. Mr Short, who favoured the devolution of some economic powers, received little support even from the Scottish and Welsh Secretaries of State. As a result the Treasury attempted to persuade the Cabinet to reject any hint of devolution of economic powers. In March 1975 a Treasury paper pinpointing the difficulties of devolution (especially of economic powers) was leaked to the press. To make such a leak is the time-honoured last-ditch manoeuvre of a dissatisfied politician or civil servant who wishes to create public pressure against a decision which he fears is about to be made in private. The Treasury paper was an attempt to awaken opposition to devolution. Its premature leaking had the opposite effect. The Prime Minister stood up against his Chancellor (Mr Healey) and asserted that there was no question of going back now. Most of the Cabinet was unmoved. The Home Secretary sat through the proceedings reading his copy of the *Economist*. Wilson's intervention – which had been prompted by the fear of losing parliamentary seats in Scotland – saved the day for the devolutionists.

The ironies here are manifest. The devolutionists possessed one big weapon: the fear of losing seats at the next election. This they could and did successfully use to stop their position being overwhelmed altogether. But they were often outmanoeuvred on matters of detail because they possessed few other weapons. When it came to detail – and collectively detail is nearly all – the anti-devolutionists had all the important weapons.

Against this it may be objected that Lord Crowther-Hunt was a member of the Constitution Unit and, given his background on the Kilbrandon Commission and his access to the Prime Minister's ear, he ought to have been able to strengthen the devolutionists within Whitehall. Lord Crowther-Hunt, however, has written of his own weakness at the time in a passage which deserves repetition:

> ... I joined in the deliberations of those committees and was present at their meetings – but, let me stress again, no ministers were present ...   I got the committees to widen the range of options they were considering, I think I was also able to make them appreciate more fully what was actually involved in the different schemes of devolution recommended in the (Kilbrandon) reports. ...   But I do not think I was able to affect significantly their recommendations and judgements – with most of which I disagreed. But the essential point I am making here is that, for months, these committees were meeting to assess devolution issues and, in the end, they produced reports ... in the early summer of 1974, all pointing in a particular direction. ...   Most ministers, in fact, certainly could not challenge these reports – or even agree with them on the basis of a detailed and realistic understanding of the issues involved. Bear in mind, too, that all the ministers were being separately briefed by their own departmental civil servants to accept, in effect, the analyses of these interdepartmental civil service committees ... before the September 1974 white paper which committed the government to broad, but specific schemes of devolution to Scotland and Wales, ministers had collectively had, at most, only two or three meetings, lasting altogether a mere handful of hours, to consider a civil service presentation which had taken months to prepare and well over 1,000 civil service man-hours in inter-departmental committee meetings alone to hammer out.   ... you can see what a very unequal balance of power situation this was.[7]

The effect was that once the Labour Party decided that it wanted a form of devolution, and was forced by the Scottish and Welsh sections of the party to back elected chambers with, in the Scottish case, legislative powers, all the rest of the decisions about the eventual Bill were made by civil servants.

There is nothing improper about this. It is obvious that the politicians involved lacked the time and, with the exception of Crowther-Hunt, the sympathy or the interest to play any more active role in the preparation of the Bill. It is also clear that only the civil service had a precise enough an idea of how government operated to prepare a White Paper which, in effect, disentangled the operations of government in Scotland and Wales and divided them into two categories, those which could be devolved and those which could not. Nevertheless, many of the difficulties which the Government's plans subsequently ran into are directly traceable to the way in which they were drawn up. The plans, especially in the next White Paper, *Our Changing Democracy*, had the sort of defects which one might expect from the work of civil servants.

This White Paper was not published until November 1975. It was much delayed. Before it was published, in July of that year, the Government announced that it would build up the economic powers of the Scottish and Welsh Offices and began the formal operation of the Welsh Development Agency and the Scottish Development Agency. This fulfilled a promise to the Welsh and Scottish Parties that the Government would do something for the economies of those countries. Since neither Assembly was intended to have any important economic functions, this further piece of regionalisation looked like an attempt to build up the Welsh and Scottish Offices so that they would still have some powerful functions after the creation of the Assemblies, as well as a way of reminding the separatists that the British Government was still providing their countries with economic benefits. If this was the intention behind the creation of the WDA and the SDA it failed. By this point the appetites of the devolutionists had been whetted so that they wanted their Assemblies to have power over as many subjects as possible. No sooner were the two development agencies created than the devolutionists both within and outside the Labour Party began to demand that control over them be granted to the Assemblies.

The Government produced its proposals in *Our Changing Democracy: Devolution to Scotland and Wales* on Thursday 27 November 1975. It gave 'embargoed' copies of its White Paper to the editors of the Scottish and Welsh newspapers before the official date of publication. It also introduced the ideas to the press in Edinburgh and Cardiff – not London. This was an extension of the normal practice whereby lobby correspondents are told about government proposals in advance so that they can digest them before questioning government spokesmen. If this procedure was an attempt to gain a good press it failed immediately. Indeed, when some of the Scottish and Welsh editors and their correspondents divulged the contents of the White Paper to backbench MPs before the publication date, many of the pro-devolution maximalists were enraged by the Assemblies' lack of 'economic teeth'. Specifically, there was no promise to devolve control over the SDA or the WDA. This decision was used as a measure of the Government's intention to devolve serious economic powers. It was foolish of the Government not to foresee that this would happen.

In England the general reaction, particularly in the popular press (which now awoke to the imminence of devolution for the first time) was that the White Paper offered too much and would lead to the break-up of the UK. In Scotland, the general reaction was the reverse. The proposals were 'not enough'. Some publishing groups had it both ways. The *Mirror* group's respective Scottish and English papers played to the prejudices of their audiences. The *Daily Record* told Scots: 'We were *PROMISED* more now, we want more'; the *Mirror* told the English (and Welsh) 'It's the least that could be offered and also the most.' It is unwise to exaggerate the importance of this, but it is worth noting that the Government suffered the worst of both worlds. In trying to appease the Scots, it infuriated both them and the English. The publication of *Our Changing Democracy* was not a good moment for the United Kingdom.

Even at this point the Government announced that it was open to further submissions about the detail of the proposals and said that it hoped to produce a draft Bill in the Spring of 1976 which could be put to Parliament in the 1976/77 session. In the first paragraph of the section entitled 'The Government's approach', the Government stated what was to become its catch-phrase throughout the whole debate: it wanted to maintain the 'political and economic unity' of the United Kingdom. This phrase was never explained. It came to be the shibboleth of those who wanted not to devolve something.

Our Changing Democracy proposed to create a directly elected Scottish Assembly of 142 members (distributed to favour the larger parliamentary constituencies), which would have both legislative and executive authority in certain areas of policy. Executive authority – the ability to operate government policy under the law – would be devolved to the Assembly's Executive, not to the Assembly itself. The importance of this distinction went unnoticed for some time. The Executive would be formed after each election, the Chief Executive being someone who could carry policy through the Assembly. Usually he or she would be the leader of the majority or the largest party. The Assembly would be able to make detailed regulations (secondary legislation or statutory instruments) under its own laws or, in some cases, for the laws passed by Westminster as they applied to Scotland.

The Government were, not unreasonably, worried that the Assembly might pass laws on subjects which had not been devolved. It recommended that all proposed laws be sent to the Secretary of State for Scotland, who would continue to be a member of the British cabinet. He would consider whether the proposal was within or outside (*ultra vires*) the Assembly's competence. The Government had not made up its mind whether those Assembly Bills to which it did not object might still be open to challenge in the courts. Could private citizens claim in court that an Assembly Bill was *ultra vires* with a view to having it ruled invalid? The Government also wished to reserve to itself the right to declare an executive action of the Scottish Executive invalid if it wished. It even suggested that it might wish to reserve the power to overrule such an action if it was felt to be unacceptable on policy grounds. In other words, a Conservative British government could – indeed, for party political reasons, might well – overrule each of the executive actions of a Socialist Executive on, say, council housing.

Our Changing Democracy insisted that the Scottish Assembly establish a series of subject committees – one for each of the areas of the Assembly's responsibility – which were to be composed of Assembly members of the various parties in proportion to their number in the Assembly. The Executive would be required to consult the relevant committee on any legislation it proposed. This was the kind of control over the executive by the legislature which many MPs and other reformers had been trying to get governments at Westminster to accept without success. It seemed just a bit hard to force the new Scottish Executive to labour under constraints which British Cabinets had refused for themselves.

Kilbrandon had recommended a separate civil service for the Assembly. As we have seen, the Government had been thinking along these lines as recently as June 1974. However, in one of the White Paper's most telling provisions, it proposed that Assembly civil servants be part of the British civil service. The argument revealed much:

82. There are however strong arguments for maintaining a unified service. It would help the consultation and co-operation on which the success of devolution will heavily depend.[8]

It would be churlish to deny that, taken at face value, this statement is correct: the success of devolution would depend heavily on co-operation between civil servants. But there is more to the statement than that. The Government's proposals were built on the assumption that civil servants would be able to forestall many of the potential conflicts between the Assembly and Westminster.

The import of this became startlingly clear when the White Paper came to discuss the financing of the Assembly. It proposed that the Assembly be financed by a block grant and further that the Assembly be allowed to levy a surcharge on the rates. This would mean that the level of the block grant would become the biggest political issue in Scottish politics each year. The Chief Executive (as it was then proposed to call him) of the Scottish Assembly would fly to London and have a well publicised meeting with the Chancellor at which he would succeed in raising the amount of the block grant by a small margin. This would enable him to return to Scotland having shown that he could wring the last penny out of the skinflint Chancellor of the Exchequer and the Prime Minister. The Chief Executive's claims would be greater if he were in a party other than the Prime Minister's. But the White Paper didn't see it this way at all. It envisaged plugging the expenditure plans of the Assembly into the British Government's Public Expenditure Survey Committee as if the Assembly were just another British Ministry. The White Paper said:

99. The government accordingly intend that the Scottish public expenditure should be settled as part of the annual public review for the United Kingdom as a whole.[9]

This is to say that the decision would be made within the Treasury, with the co-operation of those members of the British civil service who happened to be working for the Assembly at the moment – and then perhaps marginally adjusted by their political masters in the way the Cabinet makes marginal adjustments to the present proposals of the Treasury. This proposal was one of the clearest signs that the White Paper had been prepared, as Lord Crowther-Hunt asserted, by civil servants who hoped to carry on with as little change as possible.

The problem with this proposal was that the existing system worked because all of the members of the Cabinet – i.e. all the politicians whose assent was needed – were members of the same party. The parties performed the essential constitutional role of presenting the policies of the Government to the people as if they were a coherent whole agreed to by all members of the Government. This presentation made it impossible for outsiders to set one Cabinet member against another. But once an Assembly was created, there could be no guarantee that this system would survive. It was certainly possible that the Assembly and the House of Commons would have majorities of different parties. What would happen then? The two governing parties would disagree on many policies. The Government's proposal was that the whole work of producing agreement fall on the civil service. In truth, this would have been possible only if the Assembly Executive had been so supine as to accept everything the civil service told them; and that was unlikely. To put it another way, the proposals overloaded the civil service and would have led to much trouble if enacted.

The Government proposed to devolve control over most of the non-economic powers of the Scottish Office and some other domestic functions. It proposed to give the Assembly control over two of the SDA's functions, environmental control and factory building. The other economic functions of the SDA could not be devolved because of the need to 'preserve economic unity'. Half the members of the Board of the SDA would be appointed by the Scottish administration. The Assembly would take responsibility for the Highlands and Islands Development Board, and would have power to nominate to the Boards of many other bodies the members currently appointed by the Secretary of State.

The Welsh Assembly proposed in the White Paper would be directly elected and there would be an average of two Assembly members for each parliamentary seat. As with the Scottish Assembly, Assembly members would be elected by the first-past-the-post electoral system. But it would be very like a large local authority. Power would be invested in the entire authority – not in the Executive as in the Scottish case – and the Assembly would have executive authority only. It could not make the legislation it would be putting into effect. It would have a series of subject committees, the membership of which would be broadly based. Each committee would have both a Chairman, who would be a neutral figure, and an executive member. This member would meet with the executive members of the other committees as an Executive Committee. This committee would presumably be made up entirely of members of one party; and that presumably would nearly always be Labour.

The same provision as for Scotland in the matter of delegated legislation and reserve powers would apply. The Welsh Assembly would not have its own civil service. It would be supported by a block grant and, possibly, by a surcharge on the local rate. The subjects of Assembly control would be similar to the Scottish Assembly's, save that the former body would have considerable responsibility for the law (courts, police) while the Welsh Assembly would not. The WDA would be divided in the same way as the SDA. The Welsh Assembly would be responsible for the welfare of the Welsh language – this power had no correlative in Scotland.

The Government's idea was that the Secretaries of State for Wales and Scotland would continue to be responsible for the regional economic policies of their countries. This, it was hoped, would give them plenty of work and make them serious forces in Wales and Scotland. The Secretaries of State would also carry responsibility for the general supervision of the Assemblies. They would have to decide in the case of each proposed piece of Scottish legislation, and for each Scottish and Welsh Assembly policy whether to overrule it. The Secretaries of State would also play a crucial part in the negotiations over the block grant. The devolutionists complained that the Assemblies had been given no effective economic powers. The anti-devolutionists thought the Assemblies would be so strong as to lead, inevitably, to the break-up of the United Kingdom. Certainly the two Chief Executives would derive great strength from their claim to speak for Scotland and Wales. Whatever their official titles, they would be treated in their home lands as Prime Ministers. Both pro- and anti-devolutionists, as well as many commentators concerned with good government, thought the prospect for conflict between the Assemblies and Westminster had been seriously underestimated – particularly when different parties were in control in Edinburgh (and Cardiff) and London. This criticism focussed on the lack of any judicial review of Scottish Assembly legislation, and the consequence for the Secretaries of State (politicians) of interference in questions of the Assemblies' legitimate powers, the Westminster power to overrule policy, the system of block grant negotiations (without an Exchequer Board as proposed by Kilbrandon), and the unified civil service.

Our Changing Democracy was a complicated compromise proposal. It was a proposal which might have served to convince the Welsh and particularly the Scots that they had much to gain by remaining within the United Kingdom, but which risked exacerbating the malcontents in Scotland, Wales and England. The publication of the White Paper was greeted, for the first time for a devolution White Paper, by much comment and criticism throughout the United Kingdom. The *Daily Mail*'s leader writer spoke for many when he said that the White Paper made him want to 'shut his eyes and think of England'.

Our Changing Democracy changed the politics of devolution and nationalism. In the first place, it was now clear that the British Government was serious about its intention to legislate devolved Assemblies into existence. In the second place, and in the long term perhaps more important, the uproar which greeted the publication of this White Paper awakened English nationalism. All the previous acts of decentralisation, the setting-up of the Scottish and Welsh Offices, the granting of ever more authority to these Offices, the disproportionate government aid spent in Scotland and Wales, even the two British parties' proposals for the creation of devolved Assemblies, had passed with hardly a murmur in England. We have seen how few people bothered to prepare evidence for Kilbrandon. The Government itself complained in *Democracy and Devolution* about the paucity of comment on its previous White Papers. No British Labour Party annual conference had even debated devolution. Now this had ended. Large sections of public opinion in England, particularly in Northern England, were alive to the dangers threatened by these proposals. This awareness and suspicion would complicate the Government's job.

Furthermore, the two major British parties changed their leaders and this was to affect the handling of devolution. In February 1975 (i.e. before the publication of *Our Changing Democracy*) the Conservative Party chose Mrs Margaret Thatcher as their leader in place of Mr Edward Heath. Heath had not wanted to go. Harold Wilson, on the other hand, retired voluntarily in March 1976 and was replaced the following month by James Callaghan. With a new leader, the Conservative Party had more room to change its devolution policy without embarrassment. They did not do so immediately, but the party had been inching its way into an anti-devolution position since soon after the publication of *Our Changing Democracy*. There are, after all, many more votes in England than in Scotland and Wales put together. And, to put it another way, the Conservative Party which had come third in Scotland at the previous general election and continued to do poorly in Wales, drew its votes and its MPs overwhelmingly from the South-East of England. If the Labour Government was foolish or inept enough to arouse the hostility of the English, it would not be unreasonable for the Conservative Party to try to benefit. The surprising thing, indeed, is that the party did not move faster and more forcibly away from Mr Heath's commitments. On the Labour side, the change of leader opened the way for Mr Short to be replaced as Leader of the House (and devolution chief minister) by Mr Michael Foot. The second in command, Mr Gerry Fowler, was also replaced – by Mr John Smith. It was Smith who would make the most of the Government's arguments in the House of Commons.

On 25 May 1976, Mr Foot announced that the Government had taken some of the criticisms of its White Paper to heart. On 3 August it issued a further White Paper which consolidated the May statement with some further changes. The August White Paper, called

Devolution to Scotland and Wales: Supplementary Statement, signified that the Government was listening to its critics. This time it could not complain that no-one was interested. It stood by the basic outline of *Our Changing Democracy* but made a few, not inconsiderable, changes.

Each Scottish and Welsh parliamentary constituency was to have two Assembly members. The Government had seen the danger in giving jurisdiction over the *vires* of Assembly laws and actions to the Secretaries of State, and now provided that these actions could be reviewed only by the Judicial Committee of the Privy Council. The Secretaries of State also lost their power to interfere in Assembly law and policy-making simply on the grounds that such actions were inconsistent with UK policy. The Secretary of State could now interfere only if he thought the Assembly's actions would impinge on some non-devolved matter. The right to raise a surcharge on the rates was lost. Control over the SDA and WDA was allowed to the Assemblies. The Government had decided, after intense pressure from the British Universities' governing body, the University Grants Committee, not to devolve control of the Scottish and Welsh universities. Finally, a consultation document on England and a devolution Bill for Scotland and Wales were promised for the beginning of the next parliamentary session.

The Government had indeed reacted to the massive threat of losing votes and seats to the Nationalist parties. It had formally committed itself to a form of elective devolution to both Scotland and Wales which went far beyond its election promises. It had taken the measure of the political climate in Scotland and Wales and seen that something must be done to convince the Scots and Welsh that the British Government had the best interests of their countries at heart. And yet despite this political sensitivity the Government had not thought out how to produce a proposal which would respond helpfully to the political pressure it was under. It did not communicate its wishes consistently or forcefully enough to its own civil service. Thus deprived of clear directives, the civil service presented the government with detailed plans which did not meet the political needs of the day. This was a failure of tactics. Having made up its mind where it wanted to go, the Government did not think seriously enough until the furore aroused by its plans in November 1975 about how to get there.

The contrast with the previous Government's determined bid to enter the EEC is striking. Under the leadership of Mr Heath the Conservative Government of 1970–74 knew very definitely what it wanted – membership of the Community – and this determination was shared by the most powerful members of the Cabinet. Their determination, moreover, was shared by many senior civil servants. There had been, on the other hand, no public demand for entry. Indeed, the Conservative Party manifesto for 1970 had promised to consult the people on the question before entry. Entry into the EEC was the first major constitutional change fought through by a British government for a considerable period; devolution to Scotland and Wales was the second. Both differ from the normal run of economic and social policies with which post-war governments have been increasingly preoccupied in raising the issue of 'sovereignty', which is unusual in British politics – though it is a common enough focus of controversy in federal countries. But it was to be the differences between the two issues which were crucial and the main difference was that devolution could not count on the united support of the Government side when the Bills reached the House of Commons.

REFERENCES

1. DALYELL, T. *Devolution: The End of Britain* (London: Jonathan Cape, 1977), p. 99.
2. SCOTTISH COUNCIL OF THE LABOUR PARTY. *Conference Report*, March 1974.
3. OSMOND, J. *Creative Conflict: The Politics of Welsh Devolution* (London: Routledge and Kegan Paul, 1978), pp. 142–49.
4. PRIVY COUNCIL OFFICE. *Devolution within the United Kingdom, Some Alternatives* (no command number) (London: HMSO, 1974), para. 6, p. 6.
5. SCOTTISH COUNCIL OF THE LABOUR PARTY. *Report of Special Conference*, August 1974, Proposition No. 4.
6. *Scotsman*, 12 Mar. 1975, p. 9.
7. CROWTHER-HUNT, N. in *The Listener*, 6 Jan. 1977, p. 10.
8. LORD PRESIDENT OF THE COUNCIL, *Our Changing Democracy: Devolution to Scotland and Wales*, Cmnd. 6348 (London: HMSO, 1975) para. 82.
9. *Op. cit.*, para. 99.

Chapter nine

PARLIAMENT AS HURDLE

The Government faced another hurdle after the civil service had devised a detailed Bill, persuading Parliament to agree to its proposals. The Government's ability to surmount this hurdle was limited by two factors. Firstly, when the Bill approached the House of Commons the Government had only a small overall majority (which it lost before the hurdle was cleared). Secondly, many English Labour MPs did not share the Government's commitment. Even a House of Commons dominated by the governing party can sometimes cause trouble over constitutional bills. When such measures are proposed the constraints of party discipline are often loosened. For example, the Labour Government of 1966–70 utterly failed to persuade the House of Commons to accept reform of the House of Lords. For this reason governments are usually reluctant to bring forward important legislation affecting the constitution; and the recent experience with devolution is only to increase that reluctance. But for all its unruliness on constitutional issues, the House of Commons is a great body for giving way to a force that knows its own mind – particularly when that force is backed by a majority, however small. The Labour Government of 1974–79 did eventually succeed in persuading Parliament to enact its proposals because, in the end, it knew what it wanted better, and wanted it more, than the Opposition.

Throughout the debate on the Government's proposals, embodied first in a *Scotland and Wales Bill*, and then, when that Bill was abandoned, in separate *Scotland* and *Wales* Bills, there was a ghostly presence: English nationalism. The Government was attempting to reconcile the Scots and Welsh to the British constitution. But it could do this only if English MPs – who are, after all, the overwhelming majority of the House of Commons – assented. There was a difficulty here because, just as in the case of the major pressure groups, those not directly affected by the devolution proposals tended not to take them seriously until after the Government had made up its mind. This meant that the majority of MPs were indifferent to the proposals until they were confronted with them. The Government whips had to do enough to shake English MPs out of their deep boredom with devolution without rousing them to resistance. This peculiar task was one consequence of the greater degree of political nationalism in Scotland and Wales than in England.

One measure of how uninterested the English, Scots and Welsh anti-devolutionists were in the proposals is that they did not attempt to organise until the eve of the publication of the first Bill. On 23 November 1976 an anti-devolution 'Scotland is British' campaign was announced in Glasgow. Its Chairman was Sir John Toothill – ironically the author of the Toothill Report of 1962 which had provided some of the best devolutionist arguments. Most of the members of the 'Scotland is British' campaign were, like Toothill, businessmen, but the campaign also included some trade unionists and retired Labour MPs. Pressed at its inaugural press conference to explain why the campaign was being formed at this stage – was it not too late? – Mr Douglas Hardie, chairman of the CBI in Scotland, said: 'If there had been a political party which represented our view, the campaign might not have been needed.'[1] That point is undeniable and important. Labour was trying to do something for Scotland and Wales, the Liberals were in general support, but the Conservatives did not back the other side – however much, in their hearts, they loathed the devolution proposals. There seemed to be no unionist party – neither was there an English nationalist party.

This is not to say that Conservative anti-devolutionists were silent: simply that their leaders were embarrassed by them. In fact, outright opposition to devolution had been hardening within the Conservative Party during 1976. In May 1976 the Scottish Conservative MP Mr Iain Sproat had formed a 'Keep Britain United' campaign. This became a group of twenty-one MPs who were active in attacking the plans for devolution, and very active in tabling amendments to the *Scotland and Wales Bill*. This 'Union Jack' group (as they came to call themselves) were important enough to be kept under surveillance by the Conservative whips. They tabled 338 amendments to the *Scotland and Wales Bill*. This compares with a mere forty-five amendments by the Conservative front bench.[2]

But the task facing the Conservative leaders cannot be seen simply as part of the politics of devolution and nationalism. Their first charge was to keep their party together – or, at best, to do nothing which would exacerbate divisions within it. This is crucial for any parliamentary opposition and it is not made easier for a major opposition party if it is jostled by smaller opposition contenders. Parliamentary time given to the Liberals, the two National parties and the various Ulster parties came, in some measure, from the time available to Conservative back-benchers. These back-benchers could not be blamed for resenting their reduced status. Given that some members of the party such as Alick Buchanan-Smith and Ian Gilmour were strongly committed devolutionists, that others like Ted Heath and his friends were in favour of devolution in principle and that still others were staunch members of the 'Union Jack' group, the parliamentary task which fell on the Conservative leadership was unenviable. It is worth saying too that the Conservative leader shared with many others the view than an election during 1976 or 1977 or even 1978 was highly likely. This expectation only served to reinforce the usual imperative to keep the party united.

Largely for reasons of this kind, the Conservative leadership refused to come out and say what it believed: that devolution was a mistake. Instead, it claimed to believe in the principle, but to object to the precise formulation given to it by the Government. This was an unsatisfactory position as it risked pleasing no-one. On the first important occasion that the Opposition used this line of argument during the Second Reading debate on the *Scotland and Wales Bill* – two pro-devolution front bench spokesmen, Alick Buchanan-Smith and Malcolm Rifkind, resigned. Mrs Thatcher moved her party away from devolution by replacing them with two anti-devolution MPs, Teddy Taylor (a recent convert) and Alex Fletcher.

The Government won its second reading vote – the vote on the principle of the Bill – by promising to hold referenda in Scotland and Wales before giving effect to the proposals. This was an important concession wrung from the Government by its own anti-devolution back benchers. It was, however, a concession which the pro-devolutionists found difficult to resist: they could not afford to lose the second reading debate, and in any case had repeatedly told the House of Commons that devolution was right because it was desired by the overwhelming majority of the people of Scotland and Wales. When the concession was made it was widely believed to have killed devolution for Wales (where the polls suggested little support) while making it more likely for Scotland (where the polls showed a majority in favour). This concession illustrated several characteristics of the debate – and of the House of Commons when faced with constitutional bills: the effective anti-devolutionists were on the Government's back benches, not in the Opposition; the anti-devolutionists could win if they pressed their case, but this they did only on matters of principle; the 'antis' did not seriously try to amend the Government's proposals.

All this became clear in the House of Commons immediately after the second reading vote. In the next stage (the Committee stage) the Government had to defend the Bill line by line on the floor of the House. The main argument to which the 'antis' recurred repeatedly concerned the effect the Scotland and Wales Bill would have if enacted – not on Scotland or Wales or even England – but on the procedures of the House of Commons: the House of Commons was most perturbed about any change in its own rules. Much the most effective speaker here was the Labour MP for West Lothian, Tam Dalyell. He spoke more often and longer during the Committee stage of the Bill than any other MP. By a rough count he spoke more often even than the two Government Ministers chiefly in charge, Michael Foot and John Smith, and about twice as often as the next most persistent back-bencher, Enoch Powell. Mr Dalyell spoke on many issues, but his most frequent argument came, in his honour, to be known, as 'the West Lothian question'. In his book, *Devolution: The end of Britain?* Dalyell set out the argument he made so familiar in the House:

We have yet to examine the role of the Scottish MPs at Westminster. What exactly will this role be? To what extent could they involve themselves in Scottish Affairs which, theoretically at least – were the concern of the Assembly? ... We would have the absurd situation in which Scottish and Welsh MPs could continue to legislate on subjects which had been devolved to the Assemblies in their own countries. They would not be responsible to their own constituents for such legislation, nor would they be answerable to the English voters who would be affected by it.[3]

Not immodestly, Dalyell asserted:

... one of the turning points (of the debate in the House of Commons) was when it dawned on the majority of Members that Scots MPs would be able to vote upon matters affecting England, which they could not vote upon as they affected their own backyards. Like other people, MPs tend to think more clearly and urgently where their own interests are directly affected.[4]

Considerations such as these weighed with the Commons. When the Government attempted to impose a time-table measure (commonly called a 'guillotine') on the proceedings on 22 February 1977, it lost. Even though the Commons had succeeded in debating only four of the 115 clauses of the Bill in ten days of debate, the vote went against the guillotine by a majority of 314 to 285. Twenty-nine MPs abstained.

This was the Government's low point. It resulted from a weakness of will. The Conservatives beat the Government because they had become more united during the debate than the Government's MPs were. The Government's defeat did not arise, it is important to note, from a revolt of its Northern MPs. Opposition to the proposal among Labour MPs was fairly evenly spread: of the Labour abstainers 5 came from Wales, 7 from Tyneside, 3 from the West Riding, 3 from Liverpool, 3 from the West Midlands and no fewer than 8 from London. The other eight were spread out across the country save that Scotland produced less than its share. The anti-devolutionists made much of the fact that the Bill's defeat did not result in riots in the streets of Glasgow – from which they deduced, much like Douglas Houghton on the Kilbrandon Commission, that no one much cared about the proposals. Opinion polls showed a large lead for the Conservative Party. This creates a puzzle: why didn't the Conservative leaders press their advantage and demand a vote of confidence after the Government had failed to carry the guillotine? Such a move might have united the minor parties with the Conservatives and brought down the Government. Perhaps because they thought they could do even better if the Government were left to squirm, the Conservative Party did not press this advantage.

The failure of the guillotine in February of 1977 also coincided with great popularity within Scotland for the SNP (there are no regular political public opinion polls in Wales). A poll for the *Sunday Mail* on 27 February showed 36 per cent of Scots supporting the SNP. The Nationalists had an impressive lead over the British parties in Scotland. This lead was confirmed by subsequent polls. Indeed, the regular Systems Three polls for the *Glasgow Herald* showed that the Government's defeat on the guillotine came at the beginning of the SNP's longest period as the most popular Scottish party – a period which lasted until August 1977. Perhaps because it was thus reminded of why it had originally wanted devolution, the Government announced its determination to introduce new Bills in the following session. This, after negotiations with the Liberals to gain their support, the Government did on 4 November 1977. By then it was a minority government carrying on thanks to a pact with the Liberal Party.

In November the Government published its revised ideas. It had put the time since the loss of the guillotine to use and amended its plans. There were now two Bills, one for Wales and one for Scotland. The Government promised to allow its MPs a free vote on the Liberals' long cherished idea of proportional representation in the Assemblies. They strengthened the role of the judicial committee of the Privy Council, making it in effect a Constitutional Court, and giving it the right to rule on the propriety of the laws passed by the Scottish Assembly. Further, the Government promised to try to avoid annual struggles over the block grants with the Assemblies' leaders. Government would consult the Assemblies about four-yearly rather than annually. The spirit of the proposals had changed too. Westminster agreed to loosen its grip. In important places the new Bills spoke of things the Assemblies 'may' do where previously they had said 'shall'. Similarly, the new Bill contained much less detail about the internal organisation of the Assemblies' business. It cannot be said that the concessions were widely noticed and popular but they did betoken a commitment on the Government's part to take notice of objections and try to win support. In small ways such as this the Government showed, much to the disbelief of the Nationalists, that it was determined to enact a devolution proposal.

Some back-bench Labour MPs had hoped that the Government would abandon its commitment to devolution when the guillotine on the Scotland and Wales Bill was lost. The Government might have claimed that it could not legislate on this question without a majority in the House of Commons. It is worth reflecting that had it taken this course the fate of devolution might have been quite different. The Scottish Nationalists at least might have won a majority of Scottish seats at a quickly called election and pressed for negotiations for independence instead of devolution. But once the Government had concluded its pact with the Liberal Party, there was no question of ditching devolution. On the contrary, a reworked series of proposals on devolution became an essential condition of the Government's survival. Devolution was important to the Liberals and they could claim that one fruit of the pact was that the devolution Bills were saved. Devolution was also important to the 11 Scottish Nationalist, 3 Welsh Nationalist and 2 Scottish Labour Party MPs. By making devolution the centre of its legislative programme for the 1978 parliamentary session, the Government ensured that all these minor parties had an incentive to keep the Government alive. The Government could, and did, argue with opponents within the party that as a minority government it could not legislate on 'socialist' issues such as industrial democracy but that devolution had a broad appeal.

The second time round the Government, this time with Liberal support and ably led by John Smith, had its way on most important issues. The House of Commons gave the Bill its second reading on 14 November and the guillotine was agreed two days later by a vote of 313 to 287. For their part, the Conservatives stuck to their previous position. They claimed to be opposed, not to devolution, but to this 'bad Bill'. The chief Conservative spokesman, Mr Francis Pym, did his best to keep his party together and to prevent them impaling themselves on any specific commitments which they might later regret. The ineffectiveness of the Conservative Party was revealed, not by Mr Smith, but by Mr Dalyell. Dalyell was as indefatigably opposed to this Bill as to its predecessor. He was a Greek chorus to the debate; constantly on his feet demanding information and answers both from the Government and from the Conservatives. He demanded that Pym state his party's position. He put the question every night. Pym had no answer save the thin formula of 'all-party talks'. Dalyell would have welcomed a statement from Pym of what the Conservative Party believed. He never got it. It was difficult to rally the 'antis' to that blank banner. A bolder statement from the Conservative front bench and a more courageous strategy might have changed everything.

For their part, the Nationalists voted dutifully with the Government but added little to the debate. They also provided Dalyell and the Union Jack group with easy targets, for each time Dalyell said that devolution would lead to the break-up of the UK, the Nationalists, and particularly Mrs Margaret Bain, would gleefully nod their heads.

The passage of the Scotland and Wales Bills through the House of Commons provided the Nationalist parties with a marvellous opportunity to create propaganda for their cause in their home nations. Here at last, before the assembled Parliament, with the press standing by, they might have demonstrated day after day that they and only they understood the wants and needs of their countrymen. In the event this opportunity was allowed to pass. The contribution of the Nationalist MPs – particularly the Scottish National Party's MPs (whose Bill received more parliamentary time and more attention than the Wales Bill) – was negligible. When the debate was finished not one SNP Member had gained the respect of the House and none had improved his or her reputation in Scotland: the party lost an unrepeatable chance. As it happened, the Nationalists lost popularity (as measured in the opinion polls) during the period in which the Scotland Bill and the Wales Bill were being debated in the House of Commons. The Scottish Nationalists let ex-Labour MP Jim Sillars (who had formed his own party, the Scottish Labour Party) make all their speeches for them. The greater truth is that the National parties had been outmanoeuvred by the Labour Party. In Parliament Labour had made devolution its own. The Sottish Nationalists, in their zeal to be seen to be forcing the pace, had decided (in May 1977) to campaign for independence at the next election. This commitment was made when they thought Labour would never legislate devolution and made it impossible for them to take a whole-hearted part in the Goverment's battles in the House of Commons. In its turn this mistake enabled the Government and the Conservative Party to isolate the Nationalists as 'separatists'. There is little enough support for 'separation' within Scotland or Wales. Only about half even of the SNP supporters want it. The Nationalists had underestimated their foe.

The Government suffered a number of defeats in Parliament, but none which affected the substance of the Scotland Bill. In the most significant they were forced to accept a '40 per cent rule' on the referenda (i.e. the House would not vote to bring the Acts into effect unless 40 per cent of the electorate of Scotland and Wales voted 'Yes'). This infuriated the SNP. Its leader accused the Government on the night the '40 per cent rule' passed of failing in its attempt to put devolution on the statute book. He said: 'Tonight the House of Commons rigged the rules under which the referendum wi'l take place. It was a last-ditch effort to wreck the Scottish Assembly. There will be intense anger in Scotland at the decision of the English House of Commons to gerrymander the referendum.' No-one took him seriously. An amendment was also passed to exempt Orkney and Shetland from the provisions of the Act if the voters of those islands voted No at the referendum (this was a heavy blow because of the oil in the waters around the islands). However, the House allowed this amendment to be deleted when the Government wrote in a proposal to allow a future Secretary of State to nullify an act of the Scottish Assembly if it adversely affected the interests of Orkney and Shetland. The truth is that the guillotine, combined with the House of Commons' fascination with its own prerogatives, kept the minds of the legislators off the important features of the Bill. Sixty-one of The Scotland Bill's eighty-three clauses were approved by the Commons without any debate at all. By way of contrast, the House of Lords debated every clause of both Bills and its members asked more probing and more useful questions throughout. The Wales Bill slipped through its legislative stages in the wake of the Scotland Bill: once the 40 per cent rule had been established (late in the day) no one worried much about the Wales Bill. It was a lost cause.

The Lords passed three amendments which affected the legislative competence of the Scottish Assembly – they deprived the Assembly of the right to legislate about gambling, forestry and abortion. The Commons accepted these amendments, but rejected the Lords' attempt to remove control over the Welsh Development Agency from the Welsh Assembly.

Yet the prolonged parliamentary debate over devolution has had effects which a narrow look at the provisions of the Scotland Act does not reveal: it has increased the visibility of devolution and nationalism throughout the UK. However tiresome English nationalists may find Scottish nationalism and devolution, it is now harder for them to believe that they will just disappear. Devolutionists and federalists within the North of England have started a campaign to give their areas parity with Scotland. The publicity given to the proposals during their long journey through Parliament has raised hopes and opened possibilities previously not considered.

The Wales Bill has had less impact. Here the Government's resolve was weaker and it did suffer major damage to its plans in the House of Commons. The threat of separatism from Wales was much smaller after the October 1974 election than from Scotland and this undermined the Welsh nationalists. They were further weakened by the movement of the Labour Party (particularly the Welsh Labour MPs) away from devolution during the course of the Parliament and by the fading of electoral support for the Plaid during the Bill's passage through the House of Commons. In essence, the Government felt it had to do something for Scotland because it was threatened there by the SNP, but no such pressure was brought to bear from Wales. The concession of the '40 per cent rule' in the referendum for Wales enabled the Government to claim it had fulfilled its promise while at the same time making it believe that devolution to Wales had been halted. In a way this was rough justice. Scotland won a concession by its nationalist voting; the Welsh did not push so hard and hence were given less. But even in Wales the course of the parliamentary battle will have long term consequences: the provisions of the Wales Bill will be a minimum demand for future nationalist challengers.

REFERENCES

1. *Scotsman*, 24 Nov. 1976.
2. JORDAN, G. *The Scotland and Wales Bill in the House of Commons*, a forthcoming Waverley Paper (published by the Department of Politics, University of Edinburgh).
3. DALYELL, T. *Devolution: The End of Britain* (London: Jonathan Cape, 1977), pp. 245, 247–48.
4. *Ibid.*, p. 130.

Part three
ALTERNATIVE POLICIES

'The status quo is not an option,' *Francis Pym.*

Parliament provided that the Scotland Act and the Wales Act would be implemented only if the Scots and the Welsh voted overwhelmingly in favour of them in referenda. When the referenda were held on 1 March 1979 they did not do so. On the contrary, the Welsh voted overwhelmingly against their Act. Only 11.8 per cent of Welsh voters voted 'Yes'; four times as many, 46.5 per cent, voted 'No', and the rest, 41.7 per cent, stayed at home. This was a result few expected – a small 'Yes' majority but less than the required 40 per cent was the favourite prediction on the eve of the campaign – but it was so overwhelming as to be definite. To proceed with devolution for Wales would be to force democracy down the throats of the Welsh people. The 'Yes' vote was also smaller in Scotland than had been expected, but 'Yes' voters did constitute a majority of those who voted. In Scotland 32.5 per cent voted 'Yes', 30.4 per cent voted 'No' and 37.1 per cent did not vote. Future policies will need to be based on an analysis of why the two Acts were not more popular.

The most striking feature of the result is the high proportion of stay-at-homes. In both countries their numbers were much higher than the opinion polls had predicted. The 'No' side so ably led by Tam Dalyell immediately claimed that many had stayed home because they had been misled by the 'Yes' campaigners into thinking that not voting was, given the effects of the 40 per cent rule, just as effective a way to vote 'No' as actually going to the polls. For this reason the 'Noes' argued that most of the abstainers should be added to the 'No' column. The 'Noes' have a point here. Many of the 'Yes' campaigners, and most emphatically George Reid, the SNP Member for Clackmannan-shire, harped on the iniquities of the 40 per cent rule. Almost until the last week of the campaign this theme emerged from press briefings as the predominant 'Yes' argument. It was canny. The 'Yeses' well knew the deep Scots' fear of being cheated by the English. By exploiting this peculiar feature of the Act they hoped to enrage the Scots into voting 'Yes'.

But even if the 'Yes' campaign cannot plead innocent to Dalyell's charge, we cannot be sure this was the reason people did not vote. It is difficult to know who voted and who did not. The pattern of abstentions in a referendum is less easily discerned than in a local government or parliamentary election. Local government returns are counted by local wards, and parliamentary results by constituency. These areas are small enough to allow comparisons between, say, wards in which council houses predominate and inner-city wards. But the referendum vote was counted in Wales by county and in Scotland by region. These areas are too large to allow us to discern any patterns in the non-voting. It appeared to some tellers at the count, however, that the turnout at polling stations in traditional Conservative areas had been much higher than in traditional Labour ones. This inconclusive observation is lent some weight by the general tendency of Labour's supporters to abstain in greater numbers than their opponents in other elections. It may well be that many Labour voters were confused by the divisions among their MPs and therefore just stayed home. If this speculation is justified we may further suggest that one reason why the 'Yes' vote was so much lower than expected was that Labour's leaders failed to explain their case to their voters. Responsibility for this failure was formally accepted by Labour's annual Scottish Conference, which, with ill-luck, met the weekend after the referendum.

In part the Government's failure was due to more serious ill-luck. There was simply more pressing news and much of it was bad. There were strikes in public services, hospitals were crippled, sewage was pumped untreated into rivers so that people in Scotland were advised to boil their drinking water for 90 seconds, and the weather was awful. Thus, despite the fact that Scotland and Wales teemed with journalists from places as far apart as Amsterdam and Montreal, news about the campaign often came well down the order of the nightly Scottish and Welsh television and radio broadcasts. There was no official information leaflet and, because the parties couldn't agree, there weren't any 'party political' broadcasts. This may help to explain the low poll.

The referendum was fought on a party basis. To be sure, there were attempts to set up across-party campaigns but they had no success. In Scotland, for example, an 'umbrella' group called 'Yes for Scotland' was established with a view to becoming the authoritative co-ordinating group. It was a mismanaged shambles. The group had no senior Conservative among its members and only one important

Labour figure, John P. Mackintosh. Mackintosh died before the campaign began. In the meantime, the fact that the group had formed without leading Conservative devolutionists such as Alick Buchanan-Smith or leading Liberals such as Russell Johnstone and David Steel, and without any sign of support from the largest party in Scotland – Labour – but had strong representation from the nearly defunct Scottish Labour Party through its leader Jim Sillars and the backing of two SNP vice-chairmen, Margo MacDonald and Neil MacCormick, meant that the 'Yes for Scotland' was seen, from the beginning, to be an SNP front. Some idea of its organisational genius can be grasped from the fact that its one full-time employee was away on holiday for the first two weeks of the campaign. Nevertheless, 'Yes for Scotland' – whether an SNP cover or not – commanded an army of SNP activists across Scotland and did put out an impressive number of leaflets.

'Yes for Scotland' did not have the field to itself. Well into the campaign an 'Alliance for the Assembly' was formed of those who had been left out of the 'Yes for Scotland' campaign. Alick Buchanan-Smith, Russell Johnstone and Donald Dewar, Labour MP for Garscadden, were members, as was Jimmy Milne of the STUC. The Alliance did not pretend to have a campaigning organisation. Instead it held daily press conferences. Buchanan-Smith and fellow Conservative MP Malcolm Rifkind bravely used the alliance to stand out against the surge of their party into the 'No' camp. The other large 'Yes' campaign was 'Labour says Yes'. This was run entirely by the Labour Party and was set up during 1978, when the party was very popular in Scotland in the expectation that it would overwhelm the other parts of the 'Yes' campaign as well as the Labour 'No' protagonists by bringing up a steady stream of senior ministers. The 'Labour says Yes' campaign had about £25,000 to spend – most of it went on posters which depicted the Prime Minister and simply announced 'Labour says Yes'. Labour fielded a small organisation to distribute leaflets but it ran out of its own news-sheet despite considerable subventions from some of the larger unions. The spirit of the Labour campaign was much depressed by the fact that the opinion polls had begun to show the party slipping badly in Scotland to the advantage of the Conservatives.

The 'No' campaigners were divided into two main camps. There was an umbrella 'Scotland says No' and a 'Labour says No' campaign. In practice the former was dominated by Conservatives and large donations. Among its slogans were 'Scotland "No"s Best', 'Devolution = divide and misrule' as well as the regrettably sexist 'Nice girls say No'. This campaign had about £90,000 at its disposal. In mid-

February powerful assistance was given by Lord Home who, speaking at a meeting organised by the Scottish Conservative Party to a press release handed out by that capable organisation, but nonetheless 'as an individual', urged people to vote, not against the principle, but against the specific form of devolution in the Scotland Act.

The Labour 'No' campaign was led by Tam Dalyell, Robin Cook, MP for Edinburgh Central, and Brian Wilson, an abrasive young journalist. It was a forceful band which seriously upset the Labour 'Yes' people.

Both sides had awkward bedfellows. The Labour 'No' people worked with Tories, but they pointed out that the 'Yes' side was supported by the Orange Order. And they exploited the fact that the 'Yes' campaigns were dominated by the SNP. This lent weight to their claim that devolution was just a step to separation. The SNP were united, in public at least, in their fight for the Act, but it was their social democrats rather than their reactionaries who threw themselves into the campaign. The opinion polls consistently showed that the overwhelming majority of SNP voters intended to vote 'Yes'. Yet it can be argued that the 'Yes' side paid heavily for this support. On the one hand, the SNP were weak in Scotland during the months before the referendum, they had performed poorly in the three Scottish by-elections in 1978, receiving less support than they had in October 1974. They therefore had fewer votes to deliver to the 'Yes' tally. On the other hand, the poor showing of the SNP in this period had removed the political pressure from Labour at the crucial moment. It was possible for some Labour MPs and many activists to believe that the SNP had been dished and that the Scotland Act was, therefore, redundant. Finally, the identification of the SNP with the 'Yes' cause may have strengthened the impression that devolution was about separation despite what the Government said.

But, such quirks of fate aside, it is clear that the 'No' side won a great moral victory in Scotland and a crushing electoral victory in Wales because they won the argument. Polls in both Scotland and Wales showed that those who voted 'No' did so for the reasons that the 'No' campaigners had hammered home. They did not want to pay extra taxes for extra bureaucrats or extra politicians and they were afraid of separation.

Support for devolution, as we showed in Chapter 6, was always thin – people wanted it, but not very much – and the 'No' side was to interpret this sentiment correctly and turn it to advantage. People feared over-government more than they wanted devolution to Scotland (or Wales). The lessons of local government and health service reorganisation were well remembered. All the main arguments people gave for voting 'No' were anti-Government arguments. This is a most important pointer to the future. The 'Noes' won, paradoxically, because they were able to focus popular frustration with the failures of governments of both parties and bureaucracies of all descriptions. They won, in other words, by capitalising on the very frustrations which only a few years earlier had been so successfully exploited by the Nationalists. Governments seem to be losing the support of the public, and popular support often goes to a party or group which can portray itself, even temporarily as being against 'them'. This was one powerful reason for the 'No' victory.

The movement in Scottish and Welsh voters towards the Nationalist parties was made possible, in the first instance, by the new responsibilities which the British state had taken upon itself and by the way it administered these new responsibilities. The state came increasingly to promise economic benefits to each individual citizen; at the same time, in Scotland and Wales, to administer its programmes designed to help individuals from Scotland and Wales. Thus the performance of government in improving standards of livings, housing conditions, keeping down prices, taxes and unemployment rates, became the central issues of British politics. When it came to the referendum in March 1979, the 'Noes' won because they were able to convince people that there was a conflict between these economic benefits and the increased expenditure on government which devolution would entail. Nationalism was strong enough to produce 13 Nationalist MPs in the 1974–79 Parliament but not strong enough, at the end of that parliament, to withstand the 'No' campaign.

There was another important reason for the failure of the 'Yes' side to gather the votes which so many of its members had been assuring the Government were there to be harvested. Labour failed to make its distinctive arguments for devolution heard. The devolutionist camp was always a coalition of Nationalists and democrats. During the campaign one heard the Nationalist argument clearly enough – perhaps too clearly, for, as we have noted, it drove Labour voters away. But the distinctive democratic argument for devolution – that the Scottish and Welsh offices needed to be controlled by directly elected legislatures – was not heard. The Labour Party, divided against itself, did not put it forcefully and with enough conviction. During the campaign indeed, one heard many Labour voters repeating the (partly true) assertion that their party had only been converted back to devolution because of the Nationalist threat.

The recession in Nationalist fortunes was confirmed in the general election which followed the referendum two months later. The SNP lost 9 of its 11 seats; its share of the poll dropped from 30 per cent to 17 per cent. It gave up second place in Scotland to the Conservatives and came a poor fourth in many seats. In the Parliament elected in 1979 the SNP's two seats were a poor return for its 17 per cent of the poll but it is the reduction in numbers of MPs which will be noticed in Westminster. The fact is that the SNP is not badly placed despite this set-back. It is lying a close second in a number of the seats it formerly held and it could forge ahead again if it can find another issue – like oil – around which to focus Scots' discontents with the Union. Many unionists in the Conservative Party in Scotland will rejoice in the apparent demise of the Nationalist threat.

They, and many devolutionists in all parties, will be inclined to overlook the progress the devolutionist cause made in the 1974–79 Parliament despite the failure of the Scotland and Wales Acts and the return of an anti-devolutionist government at the end of the Parliament. Much the most important change to occur during the 1974–79 parliament in the government of Scotland – arguably the most important step forward devolution has ever taken – was the creation of the SDA and the WDA. Responsibility for the administration of these job creating agencies rests with the Scottish and Welsh Offices. Between them these two development agencies will make the running for ever more power and money to be given to their tasks of improving the Scottish and Welsh industrial bases. Between them they have already saved thousands of jobs and created many new ones. Their work will serve further to heighten Scots' and Welshmen's sense that the government that matters to them is Scottish and Welsh government. Their very existence will keep the argument for devolution alive no matter what happens to the Nationalist electoral threat.

Out of this situation a number of possible policies emerge. The first is that nothing will be done save that devolution will be buried in an unmarked grave. There are some senior Conservatives who would not be unhappy to see such an end. As far as Wales is concerned, of course, the correctness of this policy is hard to deny. The great danger of this policy in the case of Scotland is that it deprives British governments of any protection should the Scottish Nationalists again do well at the polls. This will happen soon enough. Given the present first-past-the-post electoral system, the SNP could well win more than its present two parliamentary seats. When that happens the Government of the day will wish it had some form of devolution with which to hide its nakedness. With devolution it can always stall – argue that the new system must be given a chance to prove itself – or concede crumbs of additional power. Without any form of legislative devolution the British government might conceivably be forced to negotiate terms of independence with the SNP.

Precisely because the policy of 'no action' is so dangerous for the United Kingdom it is unlikely to be followed for long. Recognising this danger, a Conservative government might be tempted to concede a form of devolution – perhaps one substantially less awesome than the Scotland Act. An Assembly along the lines proposed by Lord Home or Malcolm Rifkind might fit the bill. It might be possible to rename the Scottish Grand Committee the 'Scottish Assembly'. This renamed committee could meet in Edinburgh – even in the chamber which Labour prepared for its Assembly. This 'Assembly' could take the second reading and committee stages of Scottish Bills. It might even be given the power to examine Scottish ministers and civil servants. Such a proposal would keep all legislative power in the hands of MPs. It would ensure that the House of Commons could reverse any mischief which a Labour or SNP-dominated 'Assembly' got up to. It would avoid the complications of the West Lothian question (whereby Scottish MPs lose the power to debate devolved Scottish matters but retain the right to debate such matters for England and Wales). This modest proposal would not require the creation of any great new army of civil servants and it would give the British government some Scottish policy to hide behind in the event of a future Nationalist revival.

More cynically, a Conservative government might also conclude that such an 'Assembly' would cut the ground from under the Labour Party in Scotland as few but a handful of journalists and political scientists would be able to tell the difference between this animal and the Scotland Act's Assembly. Labour and the SNP would, of course, damn it as weak and ineffective at first, but they would be likely to control it and people are not prone to attack what they own. If such an 'Assembly' were created, British governments could hide behind it for years, giving small concessions here and there to buy SNP favour and still not concede anything so powerful as proposed in the Scotland Act. But, on the other hand, the very fact that the Conservative Party would be unlikely to dominate this 'Assembly' might deter them from creating it.

Another alternative policy is a return to a – suitably amended – Scotland Act. The arguments for it, other, of course, than widespread public support, remain much the same. Some, indeed, of the more glaring anomalies in the Act could easily be removed. There was never any argument for Scotland to retain 71 MPs: the number could, as Kilbrandon suggested, be reduced to 57. More important, proportional representation could be introduced into the voting system – this would reduce Lord Home's fears of an SNP majority in the Assembly. Some form of taxation power could be devolved if the price were paid. It is scandalous for the British Treasury to deny that it is capable of devolving any powers to levy tax when so many other countries do it. Most of all, a revised Scotland Act could embody some form of the 'in-and-out' principle. Under such a principle the remaining Scottish MPs at Westminster would not be allowed to take part in the proceedings of the House when it was debating England or Welsh domestic matters. The 'in-and-out' principle ought to be attractive to Conservatives since it would ensure them a semi-permanent majority on most social issues at Westminster – no small prize. Labour remains formally committed to devolution and may be expected to consider a plan along these lines in the future.

But either of these future policies would face formidable hurdles. Each of the hurdles the Scotland Act scraped over will be higher now as a result of the Scotland Act's success in surmounting them. The enemies of devolution are many and powerful and will be better prepared if there is a next time. No government will want to face the House of Commons with a devolution proposal unless it commands a considerable majority and can rely on the loyalty of its own backbenchers. It will never again be possible to argue that the people of Scotland want devolution, for no matter what the polls say they will be dismissed by the opponents of devolution who will cite the precedent of the 1979 vote. In addition, the success of the anti-devolvers in attaching a referendum to the Scotland and Wales Acts has created a precedent – a new hurdle – which constitutional reformers will be expected to jump.

The British constitution would seem, then, to have reached deadlock. On the one hand, the impetus for change is considerable. In the case of Scotland and Wales there is the recurring spur of Nationalist electoral success. Nor can any British government forget that a majority of Scots voted 'Yes' in the referendum: to give them nothing is to risk further discrediting government. On the other hand, parliamentary opposition to the creation of any subordinate Assembly which MPs think might threaten their position is fierce. Members of the House of Commons cherish their historic privileges and defend them the more stoutly as their substance becomes less. Devolution of administrative function can be accomplished more or less by stealth. Devolution of legislative and executive power requires the assent of

Parliament and this will be very difficult to obtain.

There is a way out of this impasse but it requires us to take a few steps back from the calculations of daily compromise and partisan advantage if we are to see it clearly. One clue comes in the oft-repeated claim of Tam Dalyell that when the Scotland and Wales Bill and subsequently the Scotland and the Wales Bills came to the floor of the House of Commons, the proponents of change were unable to defend their ideas save by asserting that devolution was something the overwhelming majority of the Scottish and Welsh people wanted. There was no answer to this charge. And the main reason was that the Bills had been produced in response to a threat. Whether one perceives this threat (of Nationalist seats in Parliament) as mainly aimed at the British parties, as is commonly the case, or to the United Kingdom, as it also was, is beside the point. These Bills were *ad hoc* solutions which had precious little grounding in political principle or theory. All that supporters of the Acts could argue during the referendum campaign was that they were the best the House of Commons was capable of producing (and there was some truth in that).

It is hardly surprising that the advocates of change could get themselves taken seriously only when the Nationalists threatened to win majorities in Scotland, but is disappointing that the reformers did not put the intervening periods to better use. Only the minority report of the Kilbrandon Commission even attempted to do the job and it did not get terribly far. Its authors invoked the principle that rights extended to one group of citizens should be extended to all, but this was only a beginning, and in any case the lead given in the minority report was not followed by the Government. To take one specific point: the Scotland Act was all but incomprehensible, yet it purported to advance democracy. Can one advance democracy by creating legislation so complex that even experts cannot understand it? Lord Crowther-Hunt, one author of the minority report, was reduced to arguing for the Scotland Act, which he as a minister had helped to write, by saying that it was a first step and that devolution to Scotland could be followed by devolution to England. Even he could not argue for the Scotland Act. The spur to change was real enough but the Scotland and Wales Acts lacked a coherent underlying rationale. In the end, on 1 March 1979, this may have been crucial.

Saying that the proposals lacked principle is not, of course, the same as defining the correct principles. Another clue to the way forward rests in the reason the 'No' voters gave the pollsters for their preference. Government is unpopular. It has lost public respect and any proposal which entails more government will not be popular. This is ironic, for devolution was conceived by some of its earliest advocates such as John Mackintosh, as an answer to this very problem. It was an attempt to bring government under the control of ordinary people, to make it less remote from the lives of citizens, and to do this in Scotland and Wales where, arguably, government was even more remote from people than it was in England. Despite the failure of the pro-devolutionists to make their proposals attractive to electors in these terms, this is the right place to begin.

Devolution must be taken out of the relatively restricted confines of Scotland and Wales and seen as part of the attempt to make British government more acceptable to the British people. Or, to put the point another way, the force for change created by the Scottish and Welsh peoples' move away from the British parties is but a special case of a more general disaffection for which the parties are paying. There are more than a few signs from members of all parties that dissatisfaction with the constitution is widespread. Leading members of the Conservative Party have suggested that Britain should have a written, justiciable, constitution. Others have suggested that Britain needs a written Bill of Rights. Dissatisfaction with the system of local government is almost universal. Important sections of the Labour Party believe that now is the time to reform the House of Lords. Liberals and some Conservatives want to change the electoral system to some form of proportional representation. Voices are heard from all sides that the committee system of the House of Commons needs to be strengthened so that back-benchers can have some control over ministers and the civil service. Almost no-one other than senior civil servants and politicians will defend the excessive and obsessive secrecy which surrounds the operations of government in Britain. There are increasing problems about the control of the 'corporate state': the power wielded by trade union leaders is suspect even to some trade unionists, while powerful quasi-independent government bodies – such as the National Enterprise Board and the Scottish Development Agency – have proliferated. In each of these cases the democratic control of some public decision-making process is weak or non-existent and needs to be strengthened. Legislative devolution to Scotland and Wales must be seen in this context.

No coherent and defensible proposal for devolution can emerge as long as the problems of exerting democratic control over the Scottish and Welsh Offices are tackled on their own. The Royal Commission on the Constitution was a great missed opportunity. Rarely can the British constitution have been so widely attacked on so many fronts and so impossible to defend. We need a government, or series of governments (for the reforms could take years to implement) which will systematically reform the British constitution. If governments wait until the country is being torn apart, they may find that they are too late.

It must be admitted that there is an air, perhaps a very Presbyterian air, of self-blame and austerity about this proposal. At first glance it looks as if our response to the failure of one democratic reform backed by the might of the Nationalist parties is to propose a much more sweeping, more complex, more abstract and less politically powerful alternative. While there is an element of truth in this, we still contend that a major reappraisal of this kind is a necessary prerequisite of change. The great weakness of the reformers in the devolution saga was that even they could not believe in what they were proposing. This lack of enthusiasm came to be a fatal handicap in the referendum campaign. A comprehensive and principled approach to reform could inspire its advocates. It would not, of itself, create the impetus for change – but Britain is not likely to be lacking in that.

SELECT BIBLIOGRAPHY

Balsom, D. 'BBC Wales Poll', Sept. 1978, and Feb. 1979, Abacus Research Associates.

Birch, Anthony H. *Political Integration and Disintegration in the British Isles* (London: Allen and Unwin, 1977).

Bogdanor, Vernon *Devolution* (London, Oxford Univ. Press, 1979).

Budge, Ian and D. W. Urwin *Scottish Political Behaviour: A Case Study in British Homogeneity* (London: Longman, 1969).

Butler, David and Donald Stokes *Political Change in Britain: The Evolution of Electoral Choice* (London: Macmillan, 1974).

Craig, Carol 'The Powers of the Scottish Assembly and its Executive', in MacKay, D. (ed) *Scotland: The Framework for Change* (Edinburgh: 1979).

Crewe, Ivor *et al* 'Dealignment in British Politics 1964–74', *British Journal of Political Science*, 1977, pp. 129–90.

Crossman, R. H. S. *The Diaries of a Cabinet Minister*, Vol. II (London: Hamish Hamilton and Jonathan Cape, 1976).

Dalyell, T. *Devolution: The End of Britain* (London: Jonathan Cape, 1977).

Daniel, J. F. *Welsh Nationalism: What it Stands For* (London: Fayler Welsh Co., 1937).

Griffiths, J. *Pages from Memory* (London: Dent, 1969).

Hanham, H. J. *Scottish Nationalism*, (London: Faber and Faber, 1968).

Harvie, Christopher, *Scotland and Nationalism: Scottish Society and Politics, 1797–1977* (London: Allen and Unwin, 1977).

Hechter, Michael *Internal Colonialism: The Celtic Fringe in British National Development 1536–1966*, (London: Routledge and Kegan Paul, 1975).

Hughes-Parry, D. *The Legal Status of the Welsh Language*, Cmnd. 2785 (London: HMSO, 1964–65).

Select bibliography

Jordan, Grant. *The Committee Stage of the Scotland and Wales Bill (1976–77)*, The Waverley Papers (University of Edinburgh, 1979).

Lewis, Saunders *Principles of Nationalism* (1926), (English edition 1965, Plaid Cymru).

Lord President of the Council *Our Changing Democracy: Devolution to Scotland and Wales*, Cmnd. 6348 (London: HMSO, 1975).

MacCormick, John *A Flag in the Wind* (London: Gollancz, 1955).

Mackintosh, S. P. *The Devolution of Power*, (Harmondsworth: Penguin, 1968).

Nairn, Tom *The Break-Up of Britain: Crisis and Neo-Colonialism* (London: New Left Books, 1977).

Naughtie, James 'Before the Lords: The Scotland Bill in the House of Commons', in Drucker, H.M. & N.L. (eds). *The Scottish Government Yearbook 1979.* (Edinburgh, 1978).

Osmond, John *Creative Conflict: The Politics of Welsh Devolution*, (London: Routledge and Kegan Paul, 1977).

Privy Council Office, *Devolution within the United Kingdom: Some Alternatives* (no command number) (London: HMSO, 1974).

Randall, Wales in the Structure of Central Government, *Public Administration*, 1972.

Rose, R. *The United Kingdom as a Multi-Party State*, (Glasgow: University of Strathclyde, 1970).

Royal Commission on the Constitution, 1968–73, Report (the 'Kilbrandon Report') Cmnd. 5460 (London: HMSO, 1973).

Royal Commission on Scottish Affairs 1952–54 Report (the 'Balfour Report'), Cmnd. 9212 (Edinburgh: HMSO, 1954).

Scottish National Party, *Constitution*.

Scottish National Party, *The SNP and You*.

Scottish Office, Committee on Scottish Administration. *Report* (the 'Gilmour Report'), Cmnd. 5563 (Edinburgh: HMSO, 1937).

Steed, M. 'Devolution: The English Dimension', *PSA Working Paper*, Sept. 1977.

Thomas, Brynley, *The Welsh Economy* (Cardiff: University of Wales, 1962).

INDEX

Index